The Wind is Howling

T · H · E
WIND IS
HOWLING

Translated by Valerie Griffiths

Ayako Miura
an autobiography

AN OMF BOOK

By the same author

SHIOKARI PASS *(OMF Books)*
translated into English by Bill and Sheila Fearnehough

First published in Japanese 1970
First published in English by Hodder & Stoughton 1976
This edition 1990

OMF BOOKS are distributed by
OMF, 404 South Church Street, Robesonia, PA 19551, USA
OMF, Belmont, The Vine, Sevenoaks, Kent, TN13 3TZ, UK
OMF, P O Box 849, Epping, NSW 2121, Australia
OMF, 1058 Avenue Road, Toronto, Ontario M5N 2C6, Canada
OMF, P O Box 10159 Balmoral, Auckland, New Zealand
OMF, P O Box 41, Kenilworth 7745, South Africa
and other OMF offices.

ISBN 9971-972-89-1

Translator's Acknowledgements

Without the help and advice of numerous friends this
translation would not have been possible, and I should like to
record in particular my gratitude to Mr Ichiro Watanabe. Mrs
Reiko Ohashi, Mrs Aiko Sasamura and Dr A J Broomhall!

Foreword

by Dr Michael C. Griffiths

Ayako Miura wrote her first novel for a Japanese national competition in 1964. Typically, when she had to decide whether to retype her manuscript or help organise a children's Christmas party, she gave priority to the children and sent off the one and only copy of the story, *Freezing Point*, just as it was, without further polishing.

It received first prize and was subsequently serialised in the *Asahi* newspaper. As a result of this, of subsequent books and articles and of the televising of some of her novels, she became well known throughout Japan. Many people however were curious about the authoress and wrote to her about her Christian viewpoint as expressed, for example, in the novel *Shiokari Pass* (published in the English translation, 1974).

Accordingly, in 1970, she wrote this moving account of her life in Japan's turbulent post-war period. She told her own story to explain to non-Christians in Japan her own pathway from Nihilism to Christianity. In the process she gives us a picture not only of her own experience as she met with God who is real, but also some fascinating glimpses of other people whose lives touched hers. The book is above all a tribute to the faithful witness of Tadashi Maekawa. Maekawa is refreshingly human and yet so totally consistent in his Christian attitudes, a shining example of a Christian 'gentle man'.

It might have been simpler to rewrite this book for western readers but it seemed much better to retain the distinctive Japanese style and characteristics and let Mrs Miura speak for herself.

The book is a revelation to English readers of an entirely different way of looking at life, and opens windows to understanding the discreet and sensitive temperament of the Japanese whom Francis Xavier described as 'the best people so far discovered'. We learn to appreciate the subtlety of their poetic imagination, the courtesy of their personal relationships, and the way in which they see the weather and the seasons reflecting the individual's own personal joys and agonies.

All of this is so much more rewarding than reading books written about Japan by people not themselves Japanese. We find ourselves intrigued by the writer's own personality, impulsive and passionate in spite of the conventional restraints regarded as culturally proper. We cannot but sympathise with her as we accompany her through one harrowing experience after another. Here we meet reality, and God is with her in it.

The deepest and most lasting impression is that of Christ Himself, patiently leading, prompting, pursuing, revealing Himself as Ayako-san argues and fights for life. In the deepest and starkest crises of life, of human love and relationships, in serious illness and physical weakness, in suffering and loss: in all this God reveals Himself as real to the writer, and I believe also to those like you and me who are privileged to be readers of this autobiography in the English translation.

Author's Preface

The Beginning

I WAS IN my early teens at school when I heard someone say, 'A woman has no spiritual awareness.' Could it be true? For some reason these words struck me because it seemed to me, young though I was, that women certainly did talk a lot about clothes and hairstyles and gossiped about other people and yet, I told myself, 'A woman does have a spiritual nature; she does think deeply. Yes, she really does.'

This is the story of my inner life, but it does not necessarily tell everything as it happened. Inevitably there are some things I cannot write about. When you are still in your forties, as I am, there are many things which other people would find offensive, and I would not for the world say anything that would hurt others. For that reason I have used a few pseudonyms.

But, because this is the story of my inner life, I want to write as truthfully as possible about it: how it was enriched and developed and how it was hindered. The main events take place from 1947, when I was twenty-four, to the present time.

PRINCIPAL CHARACTERS

Ayako Hotta	The author's maiden name
Aya-chan	diminutive of the name Ayako
Ichiro Nishinaka	Ayako's post-war fiancé
Tadashi Maekawa	fellow-patient, later fiancé
Yasuhiko Mafuji	another patient, a medical student
Rië-chan	schoolgirl patient
Tsutomu Kuroe	fellow-patient, of Hokkaido Police
Nishimura-sensei	Sapporo businessman, a church elder
Kazue Ochi	Christian nurse in Sapporo hospital
Mitsuyo Miura	almost Tadashi Maekawa again
Kenji Igarashi	Christian businessman from Tokyo

Contents

The Old Way Gone   11

Looking for the Way   39

The New Way   96

The Lonely Way   126

A Way Prepared   146

'Anyone who has ever been snatched away from Nihilism knows that this does not happen by way of a harmless process of growth and becoming; he knows that he has been laid hold of by a higher hand and drawn across the saving border. But we come to this life only if we dare to face the ultimate loneliness of Nothingness. From here all human work ceases; here we come to — the end, but where we come to the end, the wonders of God begin.'

HELMUT THIELICKE

'I am the Way, the Truth, and the Life': Jesus Christ
(*John's Gospel, 14. 6.*)

The Old Way Gone

1

IT WAS APRIL 13th, 1947, when the engagement present from Ichiro Nishinaka arrived at my home, and for some reason I suddenly fainted, with 'anaemia'. In all my twenty-four years I had never once been anaemic, so when I fell ill on my engagement day of all days, it gave me a sense of foreboding. And when I recovered consciousness in bed I had to ask myself why I was getting engaged.

1947 was the year after Japan's defeat. Unless I explain about that defeat and my own problems, I am afraid you will not understand about my engagement.

I had been a primary school teacher for seven years when the defeat came and, though I am referring to this in a few words, it was of course a major event in my own life and for the entire Japanese nation.

My years as a teacher had been the most genuine and hardworking I had so far known. The children had far more appeal for me than the opposite sex. When lessons were over I would see the children to the door and with bows and cries of 'Goodbye teacher, *sayonara*', they would scatter at full speed. How often I had felt sad as I watched them run homewards, with satchels rattling, for however hard I taught them, however much I loved them, the best place for these children was still with their mothers. Inwardly I envied their parents. I was quite a strict teacher, but I loved the children too much.

Every day I kept a diary about each of the children, so

eventually I had as many diaries as children. When they had gone home, I sat in the empty classroom with the pile of diaries and wrote in them one by one, until the evening light began to fail.

In a class of fifty-five or fifty-six children, three or four every day would leave no impression, so the following day in the first hour of school I would ask those children questions, or let them read to me. In this way I inwardly tried to make up for anything lacking in my work as a teacher.

I wanted to be a good teacher and I wanted to love the children; so if the lesson was on the national language, by the time it was over each child would have had a chance to read aloud, or if it was arithmetic I would keep behind those who did not understand, to teach them further. I think the children found me rather annoying! Maybe they just thought I was unnecessarily strict with them.

I took my teaching seriously, but I wonder if I really understood what education meant. If I had, I would certainly never have become a teacher.

2

I was not yet seventeen when I became a junior school teacher. My first school was in a coal-mining town, and there were forty teachers. It was a very strange school. For one thing it started so early in the morning. By five a.m. the headmaster and several teachers were already there. There was no need to arrive before six-thirty, but the headmaster was always there by five.

Only last year I heard someone recall an incident in which one teacher, seeing the figure of the headmaster wielding a broom in the school grounds in the pale morning light, murmured, 'I'm sorry I'm late', and the headmaster replied, 'You're always saying you're sorry, but you still don't arrive before I do'.

However, the fact that it was wartime, and a time when the whole nation seemed somewhat unbalanced, probably explained in some measure the kind of school it was. From five to six a.m. the ground around the shrine and the sports field was ritually swept, leaving a pattern of circular furrows. Even today I can remember my diffident feeling as I walked across the freshly-swept earth to go to school.

From half past six to seven we had study time when all the teachers read their own books. At seven the staff had their morning assembly. We respectfully read the Imperial Mandates which we had received, and we sang the teachers' song which went as follows:

Even though the fresh water has become impure,
Our task is to raise in purity the flowers which blossom there.

When the song ended, the teacher on duty gave an exhortation. For instance, I remember how these remarks impressed me:

'When I was crossing the school grounds one snowy day, I tried to walk straight towards a certain target. When I had reached the target I turned round and looked back. Although I thought I had walked straight, my footprints had turned this way and that as I went.'

The one who said this was particularly eloquent in Japanese, and I deeply respected him. I had just left school at seventeen, and his words made me think.

After this exhortation the headmaster would say a few words. While I found these early mornings trying, staff assemblies were an interesting half-hour for me.

Seven to seven-thirty was the children's private study time. After that it took at least half an hour for over two thousand children to line up for morning assembly in the gymnasium and return to their classes. The school began so early in the morning, it was rumoured that by the time lessons started at eight some of the teachers were half asleep! From this point of view alone, it was a formidable school, but one can attribute it to the times.

At all events, having just left school and been plunged

into society, I accepted without question that a teacher should discipline herself from first thing in the morning, even though the early start seemed a little strange. There is a proverb, 'However great a man is, he cannot stand aloof from his time'. How much less could a young girl who didn't know East from West be expected to discern accurately the thinking of that era.

'The nation takes precedence over the individual.' In 1941–42 that had already been our major theme for twenty years. Today, if you said it, people would burst out laughing. The aim of education was to build a nation for the Emperor, so, by being wholeheartedly in favour of 'education', my outlook was fundamentally wrong. You will understand why the defeat was such an overwhelming event for us.

When the defeat came, the American army arrived to take control, and finally Japan was occupied. Now we had to follow the instructions of those Americans. We had to go right through the State-authorised textbooks and correct them.

'Now, rub your ink sticks.'[1]

As I spoke, the children quietly got their ink ready. When I looked at their childish faces, my eyes filled with tears. First we took out the book on ethics and I instructed them as I had been ordered.

'Please cross out page 1, columns 2 to 5.'[2] As I spoke, the tears slipped down my cheeks. What Japanese teacher would ever have believed that, at the order of foreigners, parts of the State-authorised textbooks would be struck out? Was there one teacher in defeated Japan who could instruct her pupils to do such a humiliating thing?

The children silently obeyed my instructions and crossed out the passages. No one said a word. When we finished the book on ethics, we got out the book on the national

[1] They were using blocks of Indian ink, water and brushes at that time.
[2] Traditionally Japanese books usually begin at the 'back'. The language is written vertically from top to bottom, in columns from right to left across the page.

language. As I watched the children correcting their books,
I made my decision. I could no longer stand in front of
a class. As soon as possible in the near future I would resign.
It was too painful to be in charge of the children. What did
it really mean to order them to correct their books in this
way? Had Japan been wrong until now? If Japan had not
been wrong, was America wrong? If one was right, which
was wrong?

Having just been defeated, Japan was literally turned up-
side down and in great confusion, and the hitherto absolute
obedience to Japanese martial law was shattered. Some
people even began to abuse and strike superior officers. The
soldiers who until yesterday had stood motionless to attention whenever they spoke to their superiors, now became
extremely arrogant, even in the way they walked. Which was
right, yesterday's soldier or this disorderly soldier of today?
This was the urgent, vital question. Because I was a teacher
I had to know. Were the corrected textbooks right, or had
they been right before? No one had a clear answer. It did
not seem to be a problem to them. They looked superior and
answered vaguely or acted as if the question were trivial.

Some said, 'It's the times we live in'. But what did they
mean by 'the times'? When things have been right until now
and then become wrong, can we blame it on 'the times'?
What had I been working for so hard for seven years? If
everything I had taught so wholeheartedly was wrong, I had
simply wasted those seven years. And then again, there was a
big difference between wasting time and being wrong. If I
had been wrong, I should apologise on my knees to the
children. Indeed, in the circumstances, just as soldiers committed suicide after the surrender, so we teachers should
apologise to the children by taking our own lives.

In thinking these things over, I was more concerned for
the children's lives than my own seven years. At that time
my class had been at school for four years. Four years is no
small part of a person's life. For them it is a precious four
years which can never be recovered. Had I over that period
presumed on my position as teacher and taught them error?

Or if the teaching had been correct, then what I was teaching now was wrong. Instead of teaching what I could not understand, was it not better to have the grace to retire and get married? At this point Ichiro Nishinaka appeared on the scene, but on the day the engagement present arrived I collapsed with what they called 'cerebral anaemia', and soon afterwards I became really ill with pulmonary tuberculosis. Was Someone trying to caution me as I made the decision and entered so lightly into an engagement?

3

In 1947, after the war ended, when I finally said goodbye to the school, I felt desolate. In spite of pouring my life into teaching I had no sense of satisfaction or pride, because I was constantly filled with shame and regret that, under the guise of being a good teacher, I might have taught error.

I was never gentle. Maybe I was always severe. But at lunch time I had shared my vegetables with the children who had brought nothing but pickles to eat with their rice. Isn't that the right relationship between teacher and pupil — when one cannot help sharing with the other?

With the headmaster's permission I had begun school lunches. There were no official lunches then. I got each child to bring some vegetables to school in the morning and also a little *miso*.[3] The cabbage and horseradish, the fried beancurd and other ingredients were put together in a saucepan, and I taught the class while it was cooking on the cylindrical stove. At lunch time I added the *miso* and seasoning and poured it into the lacquered wooden bowl each one had brought.

This *miso* was very popular, and even children who had never drunk *miso* soup at home liked it. Especially in the cold Asahikawa winter when there was hardly any food, this *miso* soup was a great success. But when I came to leave, it only made things worse. No more *miso* soup would be made for them.

[3] A paste made from fermented soya beans and used for flavouring.

It was in the midst of all this that I became engaged to Ichiro Nishinaka and was taken ill. When the anaemia improved and I began to take notice again, the engagement gift was already in the house and, thinking about it, I could not get rid of the feeling that I was being punished for something.

It was June 1st, six weeks later. Suddenly I had a temperature of nearly 40°C (104°F). When I opened my eyes the next morning, all my joints were aching. I thought I had got rheumatic fever. I went to the hospital by rickshaw (they still existed in 1947), and the doctor also said it was rheumatism and gave me an injection. In a week's time my temperature had gone down and my legs stopped aching, but I had lost over a stone and a slight fever remained. Visiting a hospital five or six blocks away made me breathless, and day by day I grew steadily weaker. Could it possibly be consumption? Inwardly I was prepared for it. Today they no longer call it consumption but tuberculosis. The word consumption was so ominous that to hear such a diagnosis was like receiving the death sentence, so in those days doctors spoke of 'pleurisy' or 'lung disease', partly so that the patients could make light of their condition. Finally I too was told, 'You have slight lung disease. You will recover if you have three months in hospital. If you don't go into hospital immediately you will die.'

At that sanatorium, patients who were told it would take three months ultimately had to spend years there, and those who were told it would take six months almost all died. It was sad that they thought they only had 'lung disease' when in reality they had tuberculosis.

When my father and mother heard the doctor's diagnosis they did not utter a word of complaint. How hard it must have been for my father on his salary, with children still in junior and secondary school, when he heard I had to go into hospital. What a shock it must have been for my mother when her daughter became ill, just as the engagement had been settled. Even today when I think of my parents' feelings at that time, I could weep. And yet, miserable daughter that

I was, instead of thinking about their feelings, I thought only about myself. Inwardly I was glad of this illness. I thought that through it, the guilt I felt for having taught error to the children might finally be eased.

The miniature garden of my dreams is smashed in pieces.

Although I had got engaged so casually, in its own way it mattered to me; it was my dream, though planned as modestly as a miniature garden. But tuberculosis did not upset me. Instead I felt that what must come had come.

4

My fiancé, Ichiro Nishinaka, was a serious and faithful person. As soon as I became ill he immediately travelled a long way to visit me, and from that time visiting became his task for several years. Some months he sent me his whole salary. Sometimes when he came to Asahikawa he would say, 'It's no good eating that', and he would buy me a lot of salmon roe.

Because he wanted me to get better one way or another, he brought me many religious books and read them to me by my bedside. And when I needed it he would instantly reach for the cup and hold it to my mouth. He was so watchful and kind and often sent me poems and letters. Moreover, he was so good looking, well built and full of vitality that they tried to enter him for a 'Mr Hokkaido' contest. Because he was kind to my younger brothers, they too were attached to him and were always calling 'Ichirosan, Ichiro-san'.[4] In short, he seemed to be a man without faults.

However, my heart was far away from him, dark and confused. At that time I could believe in nothing. Ever since everything had crumbled on the day of the defeat and I had given up all I had believed in for twenty-three years, I had become afraid of believing. Ichiro Nishinaka did not seem to realise the drift of my thoughts.

---

[4] *San* follows the name when addressing adults, *-chan* is used for a child or close relative, and *-kun* for boys.

'Ichiro-san, what are your problems?'

'I haven't any problems. Problems are luxuries.'

He answered cheerfully as if he hadn't a worry in the world, or maybe he thought that talking about his problems was taboo at my bedside. But I was young, and as soon as I heard that I retorted,

'A person with no problems is no friend of mine,' because I felt that normal people should have plenty of problems.

If he was human at all he should at least have ideals. If he had ideals I felt that inevitably, as he compared his actual self with them, he was bound to be troubled. Wasn't my own anguish somehow or other the result of wanting to believe in something?

For someone as kind and faithful as Ichiro Nishinaka, it was not true that he had no problems. Wasn't the sickness of his fiancée really the greatest problem of all? It was much later that I became aware that his words, 'I haven't any problems' were probably in sympathy for me, but from that time I had nothing more to say to him. With a heavy heart I continued to search my own mind to discover what I was ultimately living for.

My eldest sister Yuriko was not strong, but early every morning she walked nearly a mile to the sanatorium to prepare my breakfast. At that time there were only two nurses in the hospital and no food was provided. Besides doing the cleaning, the patients cooked their own food, fanning the charcoal stoves and choking in the smoke. I could not help thinking it pathetic that my sister should come so early each morning to cook for someone who had no pleasure in living, and the gentler and kinder my sister was, the heavier my heart became. Sometimes as I watched her leaving I would think, 'I am at the receiving end all the time and I shall die before I can do anything to repay her'.[5]

It was no exaggeration to think I might die. There was hardly any food in the immediate post-war period and many people died of starvation. Of course there was no strepto-

[5] Japanese have a deep sense of obligation to repay anything done for them.

mycin, or other antibiotics. My friends in the sanatorium literally died in rows. A patient who had been coughing yesterday as she cooked her rice died today of lung haemorrhage. It happened all the time.

If I did die there, it would not be such a tragedy. I could find no purpose in living. Either men must know what they are living for and what they must aim at in order to make something of life, or else they must live without caring about these things; I was among the former. Since I could find no meaning in life, life was agony for me. I could believe no one, and everything in the world seemed futile. This emptiness in life destroys a person. Existence itself seems contradictory. Consequently I could not be positive about anything and I could not help losing all love for Ichiro Nishinaka. Only one positive thing remained — my love for my pupils.

In November, four months later, unable to do even cooking or cleaning, I returned home, and the children often came to visit me. How much that comforted me! Moreover a pupil from the mining school bought so many eggs with the money he had earned that when he arranged them on the *tatami* they covered a whole mat.[6] I looked at his happy face and felt afraid, wondering if it was all right for me to receive so much simply because I had been his teacher. Later he sent me bags of coke, and this was a great help in the severe Asahikawa winter.

Moreover, my successor Ninomiya-sensei[7] often brought the children to visit me. I had resigned before he was appointed, so he was not a temporary teacher, but as I was his predecessor he was extremely courteous to me. When it was time for the twelve-year-olds to graduate, Ninomiya-sensei brought their drawings and penmanship shown at the exhibition. The boys pinned them up all round the walls of my six-mat room. For a long time I could not take my eyes

---

[6] Traditionally all floors are covered with *tatami* mats. These are pads of straw two inches thick, measuring six feet by three feet and covered with a finely woven mat of rice straw. Rooms are built to take four and a half, six, eight or ten *tatami*.

[7] *Sensei*: teacher, a widely used form of address.

off them. Looking at them one by one, again and again, I recalled the children. If I woke in the night and saw the drawings and writings on the surrounding walls, I missed them so much I could have cried. But for my love for the children, I could never have survived the emptiness of living.

Ninomiya-sensei himself was a comfort to me too, as if he knew what was in my heart. The most unforgettable thing of all was the last day of term. From early morning I was restless, thinking about it. Although the school-leaving ceremony is expected to be the happiest time for the teachers, it is really the saddest. Wasn't it natural then for me too to want a glimpse of the children, even if I had retired two years earlier? However trivial everything else seemed, I still loved them as much as ever.

It was nearly noon. The front door was forcefully rattled open, and a man's voice called out. 'May I come in?' My mother answered the door and her quick steps sounded on the wooden floor of the passage.

'Ayako-chan, the teacher has brought the children!'

With a gasp of surprise I sat up. I could not receive them all in my small room, but since the tuberculosis had not yet affected my spine, I was able to walk.

Hastily I dressed and went to the front door. Outside, all the school children were lined up facing me.

'Sensei, we have come to thank you.'

Young Ninomiya-sensei spoke briskly and bowed. I can remember nothing of what I said at that time. I can still hear clearly the voices of the children as they sang together, 'We raise our eyes in gratitude to our teachers.'

As they returned along the slushy road with Ninomiya-sensei they kept looking back at me, and as I watched them and thought of the two years these fifth and sixth-graders had been in the care of a good teacher, I was glad once more. Even today that moment lingers with me like a scene from a masterpiece.

5

Nevertheless, an empty life is a fearful thing and, though the children were a help to me, ultimately this was not enough to save me. With everything futile and nothing worth believing in, gradually my heart grew more confused.

In August 1949, I was once more strong enough to do my own cooking and went into hospital for the second time. It was a small hospital with only thirty patients, both men and women. Among the patients there was a humanist who confronted me, bright-eyed with the question,

'Don't you think Humanism is the ultimate answer?'

Beset with doubts, I could not follow him. I was not impressed by the idea that man is central. The painful and unforgettable experience of the defeat had taught me how foolish and untrustworthy men were, until I hated them; but he said I was just doubting for the sake of doubting.

There was also a very fine Marxist among the patients. He earnestly tried to lead me into Marxism, but I could not agree that the meaning of life can be found entirely within a material world. I lay in bed and stared at the white wall. The colour of the wall in the morning and the colour at noon and again in the evening were all quite different. The walls certainly existed materially, but which was the true colour? Could men be completely objective about things? It did not follow that the things men's eyes could see were the most precious things in life. On the contrary, it seemed to me that men were blind to the most important things.

I rejected materialism without even studying it, and answered, 'Yes, it would be wonderful if poverty disappeared and we had a society where all men had equal wealth, but I have a feeling that that alone wouldn't make men truly happy. Isn't it significant that, although Buddha was a prince and had health and a beautiful wife and a lovely child, he left his castle and went to the mountains?'

At that the Marxist went away.

In addition there were some who believed knowledge was supreme, and others who said that literature alone was worth living for. Others believed in free love. In the youthful atmosphere of that hospital where everyone was living for something, my life alone was empty.

Ironically, the more I neglected my own life, the more men and women gathered around me. Maybe because I was now twenty-seven I could put them at their ease, but more likely it was nothing to do with that. Rather, since I put no value on my own life, I did not stand on ceremony with others either.

Such was the state of things when one day, out of the blue, Tadashi Maekawa, a childhood friend, came to see me.

6

Before I tell you about Tadashi Maekawa I want to describe my own family and upbringing.

My father had a good mind, but he had inherited a passionate and headstrong character from his mother. My mother in contrast was quiet and 'correct'. She brought up ten children and she also took a great interest in relatives and friends, remembering the children's birthdays and the anniversaries of deaths. She would walk a long way to visit people and when I was confined in a plaster cast she would even visit my hospital friends. With my very different nature, I would upset her by sitting cross-legged or standing on my head.

I had three older brothers, four younger brothers, an older sister and a younger sister; there was also my father's youngest sister who I thought was my own sister until I grew up, and a cousin who was brought up with us. We all shared our grandmother's headstrong temperament, but at home quarrels between us were comparatively few, probably because we didn't want our father to blame our mother for them.

In such a large family, we were by no means free of

trouble, but we certainly had a much wider experience of life than an only child would have had. For instance, when younger brothers and sisters were born, even before the babies faced the outside world, I can remember what it felt like to be 'elder sister'. From its first bath I was never tired of gazing at the baby, every day. Though my shoulders soon ached, I loved carrying it slung on my back, and rejoiced when it took its first steps. All this broadened my experience. And with so many in the family, every year somebody would be ill enough to go into hospital.

When my younger sister Yoko was six, she became ill and died. She had begun learning to write when she was only three, and when she died she could read and write as much as a ten-year-old. When her hand gradually grew cold in mine and nothing more could be done, I knew at thirteen years of age that death was not an abstract theory but a fact. The cruelty and heartlessness of death brought about a great change in my way of life from that time. The words of the Buddhist *sutra*, Rosy cheeks in the morning, bleached bones, in the evening, drove home to me the reality of my sister's death, and the words of the following *sutra* also made a deep impression on me: The family may gather together and grieve when a man dies, but it does no good. As soon as I returned from school, I used to go to the room where my sister's ashes were, and open the book of *sutras* written in the square script[8] and recite it.

A woman is deep in sin and her heart is deep in doubt.

You may abandon yourself freely to luxury and renown, but it only lasts fifty to a hundred years.

When a man dies he must leave wife, children and wealth for ever.

These *sutras* found a deep response in my own heart.

I shall never forget walking late at night along a pitch-black road between the prison near our house and the school, crying to my dead sister 'Yo-chan, come back! Yo-

---

[8] Japanese is written in three scripts: the square syllabic, used mainly for foreign words; the ordinary syllabic; and Chinese characters combined with the ordinary syllabic.

chan, come back!' I would not have minded her ghost if only I could have met her.

Three years after her death, the younger brother next to me was critically ill with colitis and had to be rushed to hospital in the middle of the night. It was terrifying at the time to wonder whether, like Yoko, he would never return.

In the corridor outside the ward, my father knelt, his forehead bowed to the ground, and prayed. He was an indescribably pathetic figure. Like him, I also knelt, my forehead on my hands, and prayed from my heart. 'O gods,[9] O Buddha, please save my brother's life.' Not knowing whom to pray to, I prayed to the gods and Buddha together and my tears fell on the wooden corridor floor. I sadly wondered why there was such suffering that even life itself was filled with fear, and when my brother had recovered and used to quarrel with me, I would say 'Give me back my tears . . .' But that was the first time in my life I had ever genuinely prayed.

Before long World War II was at its height and my brothers joined the army. My oldest brother crossed to North China with the Occupying Forces, and while he was there his marriage took place. They were introduced through a photograph and the bride was tall and beautiful with long eyelashes.[10] One warm July day in 1943, the wedding was celebrated at our house in Asahikawa. Of course, my brother could not return from China, so in his place next to the bride they put his formal wedding kimono. As I watched the bride sipping the nine cups of *sake*[11] alone, I could not help feeling how unspeakably sad it all was. It was one of the results of the war. The pathos of being introduced by a photograph and going as a bride to distant unknown North

[9] The Shinto spirits.

[10] A proportion of Japanese marriages still begin with a formal introduction through friends or a go-between. Photographs and life histories are exchanged and the couple can then become acquainted if they are interested. The go-betweens who initiate the introduction take great care in choosing suitable partners.

[11] The nine cups of *saké*, or rice wine, are basic to a Shinto wedding and are shared by the bride and groom.

China made a deep impression on me. At forty-nine years of age my mother escorted the bride to my brother's home over there, and returned alone to Asahikawa, passing through Manchuria and Korea. It was then that I was conscious for the first time of a mother's strength. To become a mother was a grave responsibility, and inwardly I marvelled.

My second oldest brother was an army captain, but in 1949 he died of a disease contracted during the war. Through him I was shown, till I could bear no more, the misery of an army after defeat. My feelings were deeply dyed with the multi-coloured turmoil of those times.

So in a large family we suffered in various ways, and as my brothers fell in love and married and went to work, I came up against one new experience after another, and was forced to think deeply.

It was in 1949, when my oldest brother was interned in Siberia and my second brother died, that I met Tadashi Maekawa again. We were a large family of nine in our home. My youngest brother was still in junior school, and my second brother's orphan son was still small. In those circumstances, what a financial burden my stay in hospital must have been! I found it hard to enjoy the luxury of eating polished rice and meat all alone, while my small brothers watched enviously. Food was so scarce after the war. It must have been much harder for them and my mother, who could only watch. As I thought about all this I could see no point in living. I was a most reluctant patient.

At that time, as I mentioned before, the hospital was not well organised for receiving patients, so if you went there you at least needed the strength to do your own cooking. It was also expensive, so when I entered hospital a second time I became secretary of the TB Patients' Association. I only received 1,000 *yen* (£1) a month, but at the time even that seemed a large sum of money and I was grateful.

It was the secretary's job to compile the Minutes for the three hundred TB patients on the members' register and post them, and especially to try and obtain the nutritious foods constantly needed. Naturally my sick room became a meeting place for the committee and the patients.

Although I had no ultimate purpose in life, for the present I had plenty of work each day and was quite busy talking to lots of people. Provided I was busy, I was diverted, but sometimes I would suddenly feel afraid. By being so pre-occupied I was being cheated of something, being carried away. All the same, I got used to living haphazardly. Now I think it was quite wrong. Even today, if I am too busy and begin to live a day at a time, I think of myself as a spiritual 'day labourer'. Even if it is only a game that distracts me, still a mere game has made me lose my grip upon myself.

Just as these thoughts were beginning to take shape, my old friend Tadashi Maekawa, himself a member of the TB Patients' Association, visited my room. Many men from the Association visited me daily, and sometimes I found them wearying, but with the words 'I'm Maekawa, I haven't seen you for a long time', he removed his surgical face mask.[12] When I recognised him, I was delighted.

When Tadashi Maekawa moved next door to our home I was seven years old and he was nine. A year later he moved to a place five or six blocks away, but we still went to the same school. He did well and was sent to Asahikawa's distinguished secondary school. He was top of his class for five years and I knew he had entered Hokudai Medical School. As he was so brilliant, I expected his conversation at least to be interesting and stimulating. But first I wanted to ask him something concerning his younger sister Mikiko-san, which I had been curious about for years. She was two years younger than I, and while at secondary school had died of TB. For a thirteen-year-old it had been a remarkably impressive end.

[12] These are commonly worn in public when people are ill or have colds.

7

When I first knew Mikiko, she had not yet started school but already knew a lot of Chinese characters and was a very sturdy child. I often heard the words 'Jesus Christ' from her lips, but at the age of seven I did not know what they meant.

When she invited me to church one Christmas, I entered a Christian church for the first time. The children were sitting closely-packed in the wide room, and on the right of the stage a Christmas tree had been decorated. The junior school children sang and did a play and danced. Even though she was not yet at school, Mikiko-san was a shepherd and made a speech. What surprised me most that day was that even kindergarten children fluently recited long passages from the Bible, and I can still remember Mikiko-san's father praying. In my childish heart I thought, 'The next-door-uncle must be a very special person'. To pray alone in front of all those people put him on a level with the school's headmaster. From that day I saw the Maekawa family in a new light. I can never forget that the first person to invite me to church was Mikiko-san.

After a year, when the Maekawa family moved away, Tadashi was two classes above me at school and Mikiko two classes below. They both did well at school, so even though we lost contact I did not forget them.

I was fifteen when I heard of Mikiko's death. I was visiting my junior school teacher when she remarked, 'Hotta-san, did you know Mikiko Maekawa, two classes below you?'

'Oh yes, I know her because she used to live next door', I answered casually.

'It's so sad — she died recently.'

Tall, strong, intelligent, head of her class — her face flashed through my mind and I was astonished.

'She had only just started secondary school when she developed tuberculosis and died. She realised she was going to die, but they say she was quite composed. When she was dying, she politely thanked her parents and brothers and sisters and teachers and friends, and then she prayed — and died.'

This story hit me. Although she had been brought up in a Christian home and had gone to Sunday School since she was a toddler, Mikiko was still a child. I kept on wondering how such a person could accept death so serenely. So when I met Tadashi Maekawa, the first thing I wanted to ask him was about Mikiko-san's last moments.

'It was because she was a child, wasn't it?' he said. 'Her faith was very real.' And he smiled gently.

'Do you mean that whatever faith an adult has, he wouldn't be able to die like Mikiko?' I was somewhat discouraged.

'Yes, that is what I think.' His reply was very honest.

That day, if I am not mistaken, we talked a little about Pascal's *Pensées*, but although Maekawa was praised as a bit of a genius, his answers were very ordinary, and I said so frankly.

'Tadashi-san, you're supposed to be clever, I thought you'd be more interesting than this.'

'They say, a prodigy at ten, clever at fifteen, ordinary after twenty. I'm just ordinary!' And again he smiled quietly.

At that time, because there were some very intelligent student patients in the hospital, Tadashi Maekawa's conversation disappointed me. I was conceited and felt that the other students were much more interesting.

Two or three days later, a postcard came from Tadashi Maekawa. This was to be the first of over one thousand letters from him.

I am so sorry I disturbed you the other day when you were resting. I am not much good at writing, but I would like to help you with the work of the TB Association if I may. I am praying for your recovery.

When I read this postcard it only deepened further my first impression that he was dull. After that, two or three more cards came, and all were quite innocuous. However, for old times' sake we met again once or twice, and immediately became very close friends. Because we were both sick and impoverished and dependent on our parents, almost all our correspondence was by postcard. If we wrote on the front and back in closely-packed small characters, we could get 1,200 characters on a card. On February 23rd, 1950, I wrote the following card at the sanatorium, and addressed it to Tadashi Maekawa at his home where he was convalescing. It was the third card I sent him.

As I couldn't sleep at all last night, I finally got up and sat on the bed quietly for a while. The moon was shining in through the west window. Lit by the moonlight my slender hand appeared even paler and thinner. It looked uncanny and weird, as if it were no longer mine. Suddenly I felt an indescribable cold shiver run down my spine and hastily I shook the hand. Then I switched on the bedside lamp. By the light of the red lamp I sensed an illusion of warmth in the hospital atmosphere. I moved my hand into the lamp light and looked at it. Although it was thin and pale, and the veins were swelling on the surface, it was definitely my hand. The strange burning sensation in the moonlight had died away and it was certainly the hand I'd always had.

In the last twenty-six years what had I done with this hand? What had I held with it? This hand which had certainly done countless things good and evil, right and wrong, was now illuminated quietly and delicately in the lamp light, as if it had never done anything right or wrong before.

It lay isolated in the lamp light as if it had forgotten the sensations of shaking hands with many people in the past. This hand, which had sometimes warmly, sometimes impetuously, and at other times indifferently shaken the hands of others, had shaken so many hands that it seemed to have completely forgotten what each felt like. You can call it artlessness or deceit, but when I stared at this expressionless hand which had completely forgotten the past, I felt it was indescribably pitiable; and then as I moved my fingers on the bedside table as if I were unconsciously playing *Träumerei*, I wondered again if this hand would commit some great crime, and I shuddered.

I would probably shake hands with a lot more people in this sanatorium. Wondering what my handshake would mean, I switched off the bedside lamp and lay until dawn thinking about many things.

I could have written all that in my diary. There was no special reason why I should want him to read it, or it might have been better if I had written it to someone else instead of him. At any rate, when I wrote and addressed the postcard to Tadashi Maekawa, I was presuming on his friendship and Tadashi Maekawa probably realised how I felt. After that he seemed to notice how I was thinking.

He began to visit the sanatorium regularly. On one such afternoon visit it was snowing outside. One of the patients, a student, came in without knocking and stealthily produced a bottle of *saké* from under his dressing gown.

'Here's something to cheer you up tonight. Look after it, will you?'

As I put it away in the cupboard, I asked, 'How many are coming?'

'There's not much *saké*. With you and Kato there'll be three of us' — and he left the room.

'Aya-chan! Are you drinking *saké*?' His voice was sharper than usual.

'Yes, sometimes,' I answered calmly.

'What are you drinking *saké* for?'

'Because I'm fed up.'

'Oh, and does it make any difference when you drink?'

'Well ... no ... but so what? There's nothing wrong in drinking some *saké*.' I was cross.

'You have no business drinking *saké* when you're ill in hospital. As a medical student I could never approve of such a thing.'

His outspoken words, so unlike his usual gentleness, offended me, and I thought, 'You're not my boy friend or anything. You've nothing to do with me. You're a nuisance.' And I answered, 'Tadashi-san, this is why I don't like Christians. You're so self-righteous. I don't have to listen to you preaching.'

I reflected bitterly that a boy who had been brought up in a comfortable Christian home, read the Bible and gone to church, could never understand my way of life.

'But you and I are friends. Shouldn't friends warn each other?' As he spoke, he was watching the snow falling outside the window.

'I don't think we're that friendly.'

'Really? Then why did you send that kind of postcard to a stranger?'

'What kind of postcard?'

'The one you wrote about your hand. I thought you'd poured out your heart there, and since I received that, I thought we were friends.' I said nothing, but his words went home.

'. . . Or do you write that kind of postcard to anybody? I thought you had written it to me.' And he went home.

8

Those words hurt me. I had many friends of the opposite sex and some of them had casually revealed their love. I did not yet realise what it meant to value a person's love. If a man said he loved me I said I loved him. I had never thought how wrong this was; I was simply alive with no purpose. Not knowing what life meant, I thought other people's lives were purposeless too.

As I lay, one rest hour, and suddenly opened my eyes, I noticed the dust floating in the sunlight. It shone gold and red, finer and whiter than a grain of sand. Suddenly someone breathed and the quietly-drifting particles scattered in apparent confusion. As I watched the drifting particles, invisible unless they met the light, I wondered how different we humans were from dust. When someone said he liked me, it seemed all right to say I liked him. But then sometimes I would answer, 'What do you mean when you say you love me?' At this some people would give me gifts and some said they wanted me physically. At those times I would laugh inwardly. Was that what a man meant when he said he loved a woman? I could not help thinking real love was something very different.

I had said I drank *saké*, though actually I only drank a couple of glasses; but while we were drinking I would listen intently to the men's words, hoping for some fragment of the truth I needed for living. The positive answers I hoped for never came. The best they could rise to was this kind of poor pun, 'If you make a pillow of sand you will sleep well.' 'Why?' 'Because you will sleep soundly.' A precocious student who said he read Nietzsche when he was thirteen, and a young man said to be a prominent poet, could make interesting conversation, but that was all. In the end they all seemed to ape other people's ideas. Sartre's novels were being read at the time and everyone was existentialist. They would produce triumphantly as their own ideas things which I had long ago read in those novels. The one reading Tolstoy would speak as if he himself were doing nothing but suffer like Tolstoy. At least it seemed like that to me. Yet, because I enjoyed talking with men more than women, there were always a number of the opposite sex around me.

Although Tadashi Maekawa said he could not bear to be thought of as one of these 'hangers-on', he still visited me sometimes. As soon as he arrived, I was all set to argue and invariably criticised Christians.

'Christians are such hypocrites! They put on airs, and even if they like going to night-clubs they say anyone who goes is a great sinner and hard to save and things like that, don't they?' And, 'Christians are the spiritual aristocracy, aren't they? They stand on a pedestal and look down on us miserable people.'

It was a strange quirk of mine that when I wanted to be

friendly with someone I picked a quarrel like a child. When children meet for the first time they begin with 'Right, let's fight', and after a tussle they become good friends.

Whether Tadashi Maekawa understood my approach or not, he listened to my abuse with a slightly troubled face but made no attempt to defend himself. I thought he would probably never visit me again, after being spoken to like that, but then he came with a novel by Carossa and said with a broad smile, 'Read this'. He found me bewildered, not knowing what I was looking for, and being what he was he could not pass me by. About the recent episode he said, 'When most people want to be friendly they try to show their good points as much as possible, but you're the opposite, aren't you? You say, "You'll have to take me as I am, but let's be friends". It's your loss, you know.'

Strange to say, the friendship which began with quarrelling became a warm bond which no fighting or separation could break.

I left hospital in April that year, but the low fever would not go down and still I could find no joy in life. Ichiro Nishinaka, to whom I had become engaged three years earlier, was still my fiancé. His mother had already passed seventy and because of my illness I felt I must break off the engagement.[13] It was early June. Asahikawa was filled with the scent of lilac blossom when I travelled alone by train to Ichiro Nishinaka's home town.

Before I left I met Tadashi Maekawa and asked casually, 'Is suicide a sin?'

'What a horrible thing to ask. You're certainly not going to die.' As he said it he looked me straight in the eye.

'Oh, I'm young. I won't waste my life by dying, but is suicide a sin?'

'Well, that's a relief; but they say killing yourself is a greater sin than killing another.'

When I told him I was going to see Ichiro Nishinaka, he

[13] At such an age it was important for her son to marry so that her daughter-in-law could relieve her of household responsibilities.

said over and over again, 'You mustn't break your engagement with Ichiro Nishinaka. You won't find another person as fine as he is.'

By this time he already knew exactly what his own illness was, and according to medical knowledge at that time he could only expect to live for three years.

When I reached Ichiro Nishinaka's village, facing the Sea of Okhotsk, it was just noon. As I left the station my shadow on the ground was black, sharp and short, and I thought, 'My shadow is so dark, yet I'm going to die soon.'[14]

When I reached the house, Ichiro Nishinaka welcomed me with surprise.

Alone together we climbed a sandhill.

'I'm sorry I have caused you so much worry for so long,' I said. 'I've come to return the engagement money.'

He was silent, his handsome, clear-cut features exposed to the sea breeze; then after a while he said quietly, 'I saved 100,000 *yen*[15] for expenses, because I planned to marry you. If I can't marry you I've no use for the money. I want to give you that *and* the engagement money, so please take it back.' As he spoke he looked fixedly out to sea. Ichiro Nishinaka's faithfulness struck me again, and I thought what a wonderful person he was.

'You can see Shiretoko over there. The birds are probably flying there.' As he spoke the tears streamed down his cheeks.

9

Ichiro Nishinaka might well have reproached me and complained 'I've been waiting three years. Some months I've sent you every penny of my entire salary . . . I've lost count of the number of times I have been to Asahikawa to see you

[14] Some Japanese think that a person's shadow becomes fainter as death approaches.
[15] £100 or US $250 at that time.

... You seem to have plenty of men friends, but I haven't a single girl friend'.

To blame me like this would have been perfectly natural, but although he knew all this he said nothing. He just said he wanted to give me the 100,000 *yen* saved for the wedding, and that was all. In 1950 100,000 *yen* was a large sum of money.

As we watched the lovely Sea of Okhotsk together that June day, many thoughts passed through my mind. I should have thought about ending this engagement much earlier. I should have done something as soon as I became ill. I was ashamed at my lack of consideration for him. If we had definitely separated earlier he would now have a happy home with a healthy person. I blamed myself for my own thoughtlessness, and when Ichiro Nishinaka uttered no word of reproach, I felt all the more condemned.

Though his mother and younger sister knew of our parting that day, they said nothing. Instead his mother gently suggested, 'Why don't you three go to Kawayu hot springs?' and with a cheerful smile she saw us off.

There was no need to treat me to the hot springs when I had caused so much trouble for three years. There was even less reason for him to spend money on me, but he and his sister were so good to me and took me there. As I write about it now, I remember their generosity with gratitude.

When we returned to his home again from Kawayu hot springs, my mind revolved on one subject. I had been thinking about it since I left Asahikawa. I had no idea when I would get better. After several years in a sanatorium I still had no guarantee that I would recover. Wasn't it better to die than cause people even more trouble?[16]

I had been thinking about that repeatedly. Of course it was an excuse, to justify my action. With nothing to live for, I had gradually lost all zest for living.

Going to Ichiro Nishinaka's in the train I had thought,

---

[16] In extreme circumstances some Japanese would consider it their filial duty to take their own lives and so spare the family trouble, expense or shame and society accepts this.

'Most of these people in the train will be dead in fifty years. That fattish man of forty getting luggage off the rack, will he be living in fifty years' time? That rosy-cheeked young girl peeling her apple in front of me will die ultimately. How much meaning will all these people find in life between now and their death? Won't the years probably just pile up without any change until they die?' I felt I was more useless than anyone else in the world who was dying. It was all the same whether I died now or in five or ten years' time.

That night the *chirashi zushi*[17] that Ichiro's mother kindly made for us was delicious. It was strange how nice it was. How could it taste so nice when it was my last meal? They say people either eat to live or live to eat, but this night's meal had nothing to do with living.

When I had decided I would not be in this world this time tomorrow, I became unexpectedly calm. I felt free and relaxed.

Before long everyone went to bed and the house was quiet. I remembered Tadashi Maekawa's words, 'Killing yourself is a greater sin than killing another.' To be the most sinful was all the more suitable for someone like myself. I thought of my father and mother and brothers one by one, but once I had decided to die they seemed far away. My friends in the sanatorium seemed nearer and I thought, 'When I die there may be some in that place who will envy me,' because some of them must have wanted to die but could not.

The clock struck twelve. I counted the first few strokes and when it finished I quietly got up and slipped on my raincoat. Because it was a country village, the door had not been locked. I put my shoes on and gently slid open the front door. When I shut the door and looked up at the sky, it was a pitch-black night. The wind whipped my hair, and I could hear the roar of the waves.

Leaving the house, I walked steadily down the slope. Suddenly by the roadside a cat mewed. I stopped, startled by this piercing, unearthly cry, like that of a wild bird. The

[17] A traditional rice dish, flavoured with vinegar and sugar.

cat's eyes glowed, watching me, and quickly faded away in the darkness. As I went, my shoes filled with sand. I stopped to empty them, balancing unsteadily on one foot, and thought, 'Why am I bothering about sand when I shall soon be dead?' and as I tipped out the sand everything felt unreal.

Soon I reached the stony beach and walking was harder. My feet were trapped between the larger stones and in front of me the black sea thundered. I could see nothing. There was only the smell and the noise of that dark sea. Though I struggled straight ahead, it took a long time. I took one step and my high heels sank in the sand, another and I lurched forward. When the waves dashed coldly on my feet, there was a flash of light on the water, and as I wondered if the white spray was dancing before my eyes, my shoulder was firmly gripped by a man's hand. It was Ichiro Nishinaka.

In silence he offered me his back and lifted me. Suddenly, as if death had left me, I meekly put my hand on his shoulder and said, 'I wanted to see the sea.'

Ichiro Nishinaka just carried me in silence across the sands, lighting the way with his torch. After a while he climbed a sand dune and put me down with the words, 'You can see the sea from here too.'

The two of us sat on the sand dune gazing at the invisible black sea. Briefly he explained, 'I ran to the station, first, wondering if you had gone there.' And after that, as if nothing had happened he said no more.

The dark sea looked as if it had engulfed everything. Only the wind was blowing hard.

The next day, I returned to Asahikawa alone by train. That morning his cheeks were wet with tears, but he said nothing and as he saw me off at the station he seemed more cheerful. Then, as if for a brief while, we shook hands and parted.

Looking for the Way

10

WHEN I RETURNED to Asahikawa, Tadashi Maekawa was waiting for me. On hearing that I had broken off my engagement to Ichiro Nishinaka, he commented very regretfully, 'That's too bad! Well, we shall have to hurry up and find someone else who'll take care of you.' Apparently in all seriousness he was going to find some fine young man for me. From my point of view, it was only a joke. Why was he getting so worked up like this when it was none of his business? I still did not understand how he was thinking. Some days later he remarked, 'Aya-chan . . . when you went to Nishinaka-san's you asked if suicide was a sin. Of course I knew you'd come back safely, but it's really been weighing on my mind and I've been praying a lot about it.'

I told him about that night by the sea. He gazed at me grimly without saying a word, but soon he looked bleakly away. Much later I realised that, knowing he had not many years to live, he had decided to devote his remaining life to me. So when I spoke about my attempt to die, he had the desperate feeling of having his own life extinguished. However, at that time I was not in the frame of mind to consider what the other person might be thinking.

One day he suddenly said, 'It's a pity Yasuhiko-san isn't a bit older.'

'Why?'

'Because he has a good mind and he would suit you, so we could entrust you to him . . . but he's a bit young, isn't he?'

Yasuhiko Mafuji was a medical student seven years my junior. When he was first admitted to the hospital he was so striking that a cleaner of over sixty commented, 'The student who arrived the other day is really good looking, isn't he.'

Seeing him sitting up in bed in his *tanzen*,[1] his profile lit by the light of the blue lamp, made me think of 'Genji'[2] — he was so handsome. He was quite well-read too, so it was always a pleasure to talk to him. We were so friendly that people gossiped. It was no accident that Tadashi Maekawa mentioned his name. He also said, 'But, Aya-chan, it's one thing for a student of nineteen or twenty to fall in love, but it's better not to be loved and get too involved at that age.'

As always, I would have nothing to do with his ideas, and was as listless as ever. Maybe I despised myself because I had tried to die and failed. When he came to visit me, I would just sit vacantly. I found talking a trial, thinking it would really have been better if I had died.

One day he took me to Shunkodai Hill. It is often called Clover Mountain because of all the flowers there. The fresh greenness of late June was beautiful, and the bushy tail of a small squirrel flashed across our path. The mountain had once been a training ground for the army, but now the cuckoo sounded far and near. There was not a house in sight. As far as the eye could see there was just green pasture, and here and there a tall oak tree was standing. People rarely come to this hill and that June day there wasn't another soul there. Asahikawa seemed to be sleeping quietly below us, but the beautiful view was meaningless to me. I didn't think Asahikawa would be here for ever — and not just this town, either. I felt as if there would soon be a final day for all the cities of the earth, when mankind would cease to exist. I had read a novel where every single man on earth died, and I vividly saw in a vision the desolate form of a world where the moon shone brilliantly and the only sound was that of the passing of time.

[1] A padded kimono worn in winter.
[2] A twelfth-century hero of romantic stories.

Standing on the hill overlooking Asahikawa, I thought, 'Isn't everything ultimately futile? In the end everything dies.'

'Doesn't this place make you feel happier?' Tadashi Maekawa asked.

'I'm the same wherever I am,' I answered coldly.

'Aya-chan! Do you really want to live or don't you?' His voice trembled slightly.

'Does it matter which I do?' Actually I was becoming more concerned with when I would die. When as a junior school teacher I had vehemently said I did not want to live, it was something quite different from what I meant now.

'It's not right to say "Does it matter?" Aya-chan, please take life more seriously,' he implored.

'Tadashi-san! You're preaching again. What's the point of being serious? What are we living for so seriously? During the war I took life so seriously it became absurd. And what was the result of taking life so seriously then? If I hadn't taken life so seriously I could have met the defeat more easily. I wouldn't have felt I had wronged the children. Isn't it taking life seriously that has caused me nothing but suffering, Tadashi-san?'

For a while he said nothing. The cries of the cuckoo rang out and the sky was clear. As we faced each other in silence, ants busily scurried about on the ground between us. Those ants had a purpose. Suddenly loneliness swept over me.

'I understand what you've been saying. That's why I don't think your view of life now is right. It's so pitiful. If you can't find a more meaningful way of life for yourself . . .' He got that far and his voice broke. The tears were running down his cheeks. I watched him cynically and lit a cigarette.

'Aya-chan! Don't do that! You'll die if you go on as you are,' he almost shouted. He heaved a great sigh and then as if he'd suddenly thought of something he picked up a nearby stone and began to hammer his foot with it.

Of course I was taken by surprise, but when I tried to stop him he firmly seized my hand.

'Aya-chan! I don't know how often I've been praying that

you will get better and live. I don't mind dying if it means you
will live, but I'm such a poor Christian, I've come to see that
I have no power to save you. That's why I'm striking myself,
as a punishment for being so useless.'

I gazed at him, speechless with amazement. Before I knew
what was happening I was in tears, and there was something
human in those tears as they flowed. I felt I was being
deceived, but I wondered if I should try following his way
of life. I felt his love for me penetrating my whole being.
And I knew it was not just the love of a man for a woman.
He did not want me for himself, he wanted me to discover
the real meaning of life.

Behind his self-condemnation and punishment I felt I had
seen a light I had not known before. What was that strange
light within him? Was it Christianity? He loved me not as a
woman but as a human being and an individual, and I
decided, just as I was, to seek the Christ in whom this man
believed.

'During the war you believed and you were wrong, weren't
you? In spite of this, won't you try and believe in something
again?'

If the end of man's existence was death, it seemed foolish
to try and believe in anything again, but I decided bravely
that it didn't matter if I was foolish. I could only believe in
Tadashi Maekawa's love for me as he beat himself on that
hill. And if I could not believe, that would be the end of me.

11

From that day on the hill when I saw how Tadashi Maekawa
really cared about me, I gave up smoking and drinking. I
also gave up my futile friendships with so many of the opposite sex. I continued to associate only with Yasuhiko Mafuji,
the good-looking 'Genji', because Tadashi Maekawa, knowing his sensitive nature, felt I should not hurt him.

Tadashi Maekawa treated me in every way with the dignity of a serious companion. When we went to films or

walked together along the Ishikari River, there were never any romantic undertones. As a teacher questioning his student, he would ask, 'What books have you been reading recently?' and 'Tell me what you think of the film we've just seen'. He himself described our relationship as 'teacher and pupil'.

He encouraged me to study English and *tanka*[3] and also urged me to read the Bible. This letter of August 30th, 1950, shows the kind of dealings we had with each other:

> From next week we will study English together all morning on Tuesdays and Fridays. (As there are no notes or instructions it will cost nothing.) Before that I want you to get your parents' approval. I wondered if I should ask their permission personally, but maybe you could do it. You are still young and when the question of your marriage comes up, I don't want to cause any complications. I have no intention of being a nuisance, so I will be the model of discretion!

As you can see from the letter, he would never have indulged in a secret friendship hidden from my parents. When we went to a film he always called for me and took me home afterwards. Even after we knew each other really well we never shook hands, but he would bow politely and usually parted with a 'teacher's' word: 'Be good! Don't be too strong-headed!' Then after going five or six steps he would stretch out a hand and wave as if shaking hands — we called

[3] Poetry plays a far more important part in Japanese life than it does in the West. There are thousands of entries for the Emperor's annual contest and most large towns have flourishing societies.

The *tanka* is a poem of 31 syllables divided into lines of 5, 7, 5, 7, 7 syllables, with a history of over one thousand years. The poet endeavours to capture a fleeting moment in nature or daily life, with his emotional response to it. As with all poetry, the nuances, allusions and skill are impossible to reproduce in translation.

Ayako Hotta was inclined to lose herself in philosophical ideas and Tadashi Maekawa may have encouraged her to write poetry in order to draw her back to daily life and its significance for her.

it our 'airy' handshake. If today's young people saw it, they would burst out laughing!

Our friendship continued, but I was not interested in Tadashi Maekawa himself. Like that first day of creation in Genesis, my heart was in chaos without any certainty at all. All I had was a desire to search for something somehow, but I was restless, not knowing what I should look for. One of my letters to Tadashi Maekawa reveals what I was like at that time:

What's making me so miserable? Who am I really? Is it silly to strive after an ideal and try to discover who I am? Tadashi-san, when I'm seized with this strange melancholy I have to write something. Maybe you will say this is as discourteous as picking up a pen when one has a headache. Maybe it is my strange nature, but when I am tired in body and in mind I want to cry out. Can you understand me when I'm like this, Tadashi-san?

'Fact is stranger than fiction.' 'Chance' is so fearful — but what is chance? What is 'inevitability'?[4] The plot of a novel seems to hang on cause and effect, with its meetings and partings, killing and being killed, loving and being loved, hating and being hated — yet even all that varies with human whims. The truth is, cause and effect are so cruel one trembles. Change and transition are an uncanny indication that someone is pulling strings. Are we being forcibly controlled? What is the natural course of events? Is it chance? Is it inevitability? What a dreadful thing it is to be Ayako Hotta! Are men born by chance alone, or not? Whichever way you look at it, it is horribly frightening.

Insecurity causes fear. Why am I so insecure? Is it

---

[4] Both Buddhism and Nihilism (see note on p. 52) deny the existence of God and then become concerned with the impersonal forces which may control human life. This passage reflects the Buddhist concept of *Karma* or fate — one's life is determined by one's past — and also the anxiety of the Nihilist who denies all meaning in the world and then feels himself at the mercy of various forces.

because I am a finite being, seeking something lasting,[5] while time and the passing of time exist only in our minds and have no actual existence of their own? Yet time alone doesn't seem to bring insecurity.

I cannot grasp what reality is. I don't understand myself and I don't understand other people. No matter what I do, I can't find the answer. Ultimately I suppose I am restless simply because I don't understand anything.

I am deeply conscious only of man's weakness and poverty. Man's weakness — such a weakness that even in its ugliness one can sense the transient beauty. Man's poverty — such a poverty that heroes, scholars, saints and rich men seem pathetically ridiculous.

It is a lie to say one has discovered the wonder of living. How can a man have such a passionate desire to live? I don't understand why they lie like that, or, if it isn't a lie, why they can have such a positive desire to live. Some may ridicule this as the sentimental hero's attitude. Is it all the result of the sin of society? It is not as easy as that. Something prior to the sin of society made man unhappy like this. If he tries to live life to the full, either he is fated to end up wanting to die, or he will never find what he is striving for.

In my view, everything is wholly involved. It's all meaningless. It is the confused words and the glazed eyes of drunken men. There isn't a single reliable thing. Nothing? No continuity? Yet I long for it. Something! Something that will give me peace of mind! Something enduring, though the moments fly like scattering sparks. Many of us don't really want to burn hard. We're afraid. We're just smouldering, and then the smoke makes our eyes sting and chokes us when it gets in our nose and mouth. Isn't total destruction the only thing that lasts? But this is all confused rambling too.

Why am I made like this, Tadashi-san? I am trying to understand it. I don't understand anything, but I am long-

[5] The impermanence of this world is a fundamental tenet of Buddhism and permeates the whole of Japanese life.

ing for a world which is not uncertain. The child within me, which will not compromise halfway,[6] seems to pursue me through my whole life.

Now I am seeking only one thing — a world that is peaceful forever — but there are too many question marks. A poet said 'Be involved', but he didn't say with what. Are they involved with what I'm seeking, or are they involved with self-despair? When I look at myself I always come back to the question 'What am I really doing here? What does it mean to live? What are we living for?'

Tomorrow is Friday, isn't it? I've just received the church programme.

Tadashi-san, I wonder if man can ever lose his loneliness? The wind is howling.

Even though I was in such a chaotic state, the decision to begin searching for something, anyway, was for me a reality. Ever since the war I had been unable to believe in anything and as a result life had been meaningless. Now I had at least begun to look for something. On that dark night when I had tried to end my life in the sea, a part of my life ended and another part began.

In spite of wanting to die, I don't think I had taken death seriously enough. Death ought to have been the most important thing for me. That night when I was facing the solemn imminence of death and the vinegared rice had tasted so good, I had thought, 'When a man resolves to die he is unexpectedly serene'. Later I decided I had not even been serious about death. And if I could not even take my own death seriously, how could I take everyday life seriously? Although I had been so negative until that night, I had thought that I was at least being serious about human existence, but I found out that I was mistaken.

It was Tadashi Maekawa on the hill that day who made me realise it when he cried out, 'Aya-chan! Don't do that! You'll die if you go on as you are.'

'Aya-chan! I don't know how often I've been praying that

[6] In Japan the adult must learn to compromise.

you will get better, and live. I don't mind dying if it means you will live, but I'm such a poor Christian, I've come to see that I have no power to save you.'

Thinking about him striking his foot with the stone, I discovered what 'serious' meant. The word 'serious' ought only to be used when one lives for the sake of other people.

This led me to see that the focal point of my philosophy of life was off-centre. I did not know where it had gone wrong, but I decided to try and find out.

12

Not everyone was kindly disposed towards my friendship with Tadashi Maekawa. Those close to me said candidly, 'There's no one as good as Ichiro Nishinaka. Now you've parted from him you won't have a second chance.'

Compared with the healthy and generous Ichiro Nishinaka, Tadashi Maekawa was no more than a sick student. From a financial point of view they were as different as child and adult.

Moreover, among Tadashi Maekawa's friends there were many who hated me like the plague. One of his older friends even said, 'If you bring that person here you needn't come back again. She's bad for the children.'

Apparently ever since Tadashi Maekawa was in junior school this man's wife had been saying, 'When you need a wife, I'll find one for you,' so maybe that was why she was so offended.

But they were not the only ones to speak ill of me. Sadly, the members of his own church did the same. His mother told him what they were saying, and he in all frankness told me. It was understandable that they spoke as they did, for it was quite true that I had had many men friends and probably appeared indiscreet.

'I don't know what to do,' he said. 'I wanted to be friends with you within the church circle, but . . .' Forbidden to visit his older friend and even called the Prodigal Son by some in the church, no wonder Tadashi Maekawa was perplexed.

'I didn't intend the two of us to have an exclusive friend-ship. I wanted to be friends with you openly and above board, in a group.'

He was distressed that things had not worked out as he had hoped. However, he resolutely continued to associate with me. I was not afraid of people's opinions and tried to go to the church whenever my health allowed it.

In one of the notes he wrote me at that time he said, 'I feel I am standing in front of you like a young swordsman, with arms outstretched to defend you.'

Actually these things were not too severe a blow because I had never set much store by people. To tell the truth, I felt no one was completely reliable, and it was precisely because of the futility and meaninglessness of everything that I had even tried to take my life.

I certainly did not think that those who believed in Christianity were the only good people. Nor did it necessarily follow that Buddhists were outstanding, just because they claimed they had faith. Many complete unbelievers deserved to be called noble and good.

There was no solution to my fundamental restlessness. I was vague about what I was seeking, but nevertheless it could have been called 'God'. So, although some of the people at church rejected and even denounced me, this did not particularly hinder me in my search. Rather, the fact that there were church people as weak and foolish as I was myself gave me a deep sense of reassurance. Arrogantly I thought, 'If God accepts that sort of person, isn't it possible that He will even accept me?' And I began to read the Bible more attentively.

Some people go to church under the delusion that it is the place where the most holy people gather. But no church is ever a meeting place of the sinless. It is meant for those who know they are sinners, unable to lift their heads before God or men. Therefore, unless people seek God without expecting anything from others, they may be driven to despair. As I had already despaired of myself more than anybody else, from that time to this I have never wanted to leave the church on account of other people. I learned this lesson at the very beginning, thanks to those who criticised me.

13

Although I began going to church I could not get rid of my rather contemptuous attitude towards Christians. It seemed to me that 'believing' was only for the simple-minded. During the war we Japanese had fought believing that the emperor was god, and that our country was invincible because it had been founded by the gods. We were fearful of ever putting our faith in anything again.

When the war ended Christianity became popular. Although church attendance was poor during the war, people poured into the churches after the defeat. Surely they were insincere. After all that had happened, how could anyone be so ready to put his faith in anything else, so soon? Somehow they struck me as lacking in integrity.

Going to church with such thoughts, I was sceptical even when the Christians prayed. While all the others clasped their hands together and humbly bowed their heads, I kept my eyes wide open, carefully watching the faces of those who prayed, one after another.

'God, our heavenly Father, we thank you that we can pray together on this quiet evening. We earnestly pray that we may live according to your will.'

And as I watched each face, I thought, 'Are these people really praying before God? If I did believe in God I don't think I would be able to utter a word in His presence. If God is really so great that He is Creator and Ruler of this world, how can they come before such an awesome Being and chatter away like that? Wouldn't they be trembling or petrified with fear? These people aren't really praying before God. They are just piling up words for the benefit of those who listen.'

Yes, surely it was all hypocrisy. Arrogantly I thought that

if ever I became a believer I would pray sincerely. I used to pass on what I was thinking freely to Tadashi Maekawa, and he would just reply, 'Aya-chan, you're quite merciless, aren't you?' and say no more.

Once I announced, 'Christians are stupid people. They don't really believe, but they tell each other, "There is a God, there is a God", and then they are all content.'

At that Tadashi Maekawa opened the Bible and urged me to read Ecclesiastes. I began reading without much enthusiasm and was completely taken by surprise.

It is useless, useless, said the Philosopher. Life is useless, all useless. You spend your life working, labouring, and what do you have to show for it? Generations come and generations go, but the world stays just the same.

I had only read those few lines when my heart was immediately drawn to this book of Ecclesiastes.

Every river flows into the sea, but the sea is not yet full. The water returns to where the rivers began, and starts all over again. Our eyes can never see enough to be satisfied; our ears can never hear enough. What has happened before will happen again. What has been done before will be done again. There is nothing new in the whole world. 'Look,' they say, 'here is something new!' But no, it has all happened before, long before we were born. No one remembers what has happened in the past, and no one in days to come will remember what happens between now and then.[7]

I sighed involuntarily. I was pretty negative myself. I believed that when anything died it was the end, but I did not go as far as this book: 'there is nothing new in the whole world'. While every day might in the end be a repetition, I thought there were still new things to be discovered. My eyes were not so keen that they found everything faded.

[7] Ecclesiastes 1: 1–4, 7–11 (TEV).

I decided to enjoy myself and find out what happiness is. But I found that this is useless, too. I accomplished great things. I built myself houses and planted vineyards. I planted gardens and orchards, with all kinds of fruit trees in them; I dug ponds to irrigate them. I bought many slaves, and there were slaves born in my household. I also piled up silver and gold, and I had all the women a man could want. Yes, I was great, greater than anyone else who had ever lived in Jerusalem, and I realised that it didn't mean a thing. It was like chasing the wind — of no use at all.[8]

He went on to say that though he thought he was wise, if his fate was the same as the fools' there was no point in wisdom. Neither the wise man nor the fool is remembered by the world. In the next world all are forgotten. All alike die. Even if one is wise, ultimately it is all futile.

For twelve chapters the book continued in the same vein that all was emptiness, all was useless. My view of Christianity changed considerably, and I revised my opinion that Christians were simple-minded!

To say that everything in the world is utterly empty did not seem to be at all like Christianity. Mystified, I wondered why this sort of thing was in the Bible. After reading the Bible for two or three months I had been struck by such teaching as 'Love one another' and 'If anyone strikes your right cheek, turn to him the left one', but the nihilistic outlook of Ecclesiastes led me to change my whole opinion of Christianity. I thought of Buddha. Two thousand years ago Buddha had been born as a prince in India. He had been blessed with good health, high social status, wealth, the beautiful princess Ashudara and a lovely child. One could say that he had received all the happiness he could hope for in this world. But he saw an old man and thought of man's decline, he saw a funeral and thought of the limitation of human life, and one night, secretly, Buddha abandoned his palace and princely position, his beautiful wife and child, and went away alone to the mountains.

[8] Ecclesiastes 2: 1, 4–11 (TEV).

In effect, although Buddha had thought himself happy up to this point, he felt that it had all been empty. Ecclesiastes said it. Buddha said it. To begin with, one must be conscious of this emptiness. I saw this was one thing religions had in common. Because I had been so nihilistic myself since the defeat, this discovery became another turning point in my life. Nihilism,[9] I realised, is an empty philosophy, denying everything in the world until in the end one denies oneself. But when I had been driven to that point I found that something else in Ecclesiastes made sense. It was at the end of the book, and in my circumstances it struck me forcibly:

'So remember your Creator while you are still young'.

From that time my search steadily became more serious.

14

However, to all outward appearances things were not very different.

> Though I return at midnight and sleep in my clothes,
> These days my parents do not rebuke me.

This poem was the first I contributed to *Araragi*,[10] and it was awarded a prize by the editor.

[9] Nihilism is a philosophy of despair which denies that there is any meaning or purpose in life, and therefore it rejects all culture, civilisation, education, teaching and values. People turn to it as a last resort when all other philosophies have failed them, though it has nothing to offer in the way of hope or comfort. After the collapse of Nazi and Japanese totalitarianism, many in Europe and Japan reached this point of despair.

Attempts by some writers to find the roots of Nihilism in Buddhism and Taoism appear to be based on a misunderstanding of those two religions. While they all face the problem of futility and meaninglessness, the solutions they offer are different.

[10] The magazine *Araragi* was founded in 1908 to encourage the writing of *tanka* (see note on page 43). It continues to prosper nationwide, having published works by members of all the poetic schools. Their purpose is to preserve the natural and real in life. Many cities have local *Araragi* societies.

I awoke, clutching a tepid hot water bottle.
Can one call this moment living?

I wrote many such poems, and somehow or other when a
nihilist produces poetry something must have happened,
because he has created something out of nothing, and,
though on the face of it they were cheerless poems, some
creative force was welling up deep in my heart. It had all
started when I began to read the Bible.

As always, Tadashi Maekawa and I met frequently, and
when we met we discussed books and films — and the
church. Although some members were criticising me, their
consideration for me as a 'seeker' meant they would not tell
me frankly what they were thinking. But Tadashi not only
told me what they were saying behind my back, he told me
all about the church, just as it really was. Maybe he wanted
me to grasp the full truth about human nature, especially
my own — but more probably he was setting out to train
me severely right from the beginning. Just as a lioness trains
her cubs by pushing them down into deep ravines, I was
anything but overprotected.

At the back of his mind he was already conscious of how
short his remaining life was, but I did not appreciate this.
One night we were walking along the road together, talking.
It was late September and autumn was drawing on.

'I wonder what we'll both be doing five years from now?'
I said. 'I'm gradually getting worse. I wonder whether I'll be
dead.'

'Aya-chan, you're still young. I don't know what to do
with you when you talk so casually about dying!'

'All right then, in five years' time I wonder whether I'll
still be walking up and down the road with you like this,
talking about what we'll be doing in five years' time!' and I
laughed.

He looked at me in silence and then said, 'Aya-chan, you
mustn't go on teasing me, because I only want you to learn
to stand on your own two feet without relying on anybody
else.'

He spoke each word with deep feeling, but I failed to grasp what he meant and enquired, 'Oh! Does that mean you won't always be friends with me?'

He had a girl friend at that time. She was not his special sweetheart, but until he became friendly with me they had written poetry together and shared the same faith. She was intelligent, attractive and a very suitable match for him. Had he got fed up with me because I was so thick-headed? Well, that was all right. It would be better if he did return to his own world, because as long as he associated with me he had nothing but trouble with the church members.

When I said this he gave me such a sad smile and said again so earnestly, 'Aya-chan, you must learn what it means to stand on your own feet. I'm just your prop until you can stand alone. Don't you see?'

But though I understood what he was saying, I failed to grasp what he meant.

The next day there was a letter from him.

When I'm in trouble and sad, it's a principle of mine to fix my mind on something else. The hero of *Memoirs of Marte* used to relax in the museum to avoid sadness and depression. As there is no museum in Asahikawa, I shall try going to the library, and I have decided to go there as much as possible this month.

Even after this letter I did not understand why he felt so lonely and sad. Now when I recall his thoughts at that time I believe my lack of sympathy was the cause, and I am sorry that I did not appreciate it then. The cavity in his lungs was steadily driving him to his death. At first glance he seemed healthy. Tuberculosis affects each person so differently, they say that one patient needs ten doctors. In my case I had a slight temperature and night sweats and I was very thin, my shoulders were soon stiff and I tired easily.

Once he had remarked when we met, 'I was just thinking there are some pretty skinny people around, and when I got nearer I realised it was you! It made me feel so miserable.'

I was so thin it had upset him. But he had no temperature, he weighed over nine stone, and he did not get tired easily. He was strong enough to walk three or four miles without tiring, and his shoulders never ached, yet whereas I had no cough, he had to stop as we walked along the road, doubled up with coughing. At any rate, because he looked healthy and was strong, his illness did not seem as severe as mine, so I felt his depression was merely emotional.

He was for ever writing letters. He lived a quarter of a mile away, but although we met daily he also wrote to me every day. Time after time his letters arrived as we sat talking in my home. His face would redden as he laughingly called it 'letter mania'. But I think every letter carried his parting words to me.

15

When I broke off my friendship with most of my men friends, I kept it up with Yasuhiko Mafuji, and he sometimes visited me at home. He was no less nihilistic than I was. While scarcely a prodigy, he was a student who had shown some flashes of genius. There was, however, something strange about him. At times he was gay, at other times quiet. When he drank his tea, savouring the aroma, the design of the cup concealed as he clasped it in both hands, there was an elegance about him, a kind of feminine sensitivity not to be found even in my female friends. When we were together it soothed me.

He was a real nihilist and often said, 'I'm not the sort of person who will ever fall in love.'

I wondered if he had fallen madly in love in the past and the wound had not yet healed. He was quite different from Tadashi Maekawa who was always trying to be kind to other people.

One day he invited me out for a walk. The chrysanthemums were in flower and it was a day to enjoy. He seemed to be overcome with loneliness and more talkative than usual, but before we had gone a mile he gradually grew silent. He was strikingly good-looking and some workmen saw us and shouted after us. I don't think this was the reason for his silence, but suddenly he stopped and said, 'I'm sorry—but would you mind going home alone from here?'

He was quite different from Tadashi Maekawa who always came without fail to fetch me, and saw me home afterwards. But Yasuhiko Mafuji took me out because he was lonely, and then packed me off because he became so disgusted with himself, and I found his self-centredness more intriguing. Did the difference lie ultimately in the fact that Tadashi Maekawa was two years older than I and Yasuhiko Mafuji seven years younger? I felt that if I had only associated with Tadashi Maekawa I would not have had this maternal feeling.

One such day, he said in his usual quiet voice, 'When I finish university I think I'll be a high school teacher somewhere. I wonder which town would be best?'

'Well, wouldn't a seaside town be nice? They say the climate around Abuta is good.'

'All right, I'll live in Abuta! Will you come with me?' His words took me by surprise.

'Am I to go too?'

'Yes, that's why I asked you which town you would like.'

'But . . .' I couldn't digest such a hare-brained idea.

'I never ever want to marry and because you're ill, you probably won't marry either. Don't you think it would be a good idea to spend our lives as friends under one roof . . . not as a married couple or as lovers?'

'Well — yes. But I don't know if I can cook or not. I haven't been able to get rid of this fever recently.'

'That doesn't matter. It's fine if we can just be together under one roof.' Merely daydreaming about this life seemed to make him happy.

When I told my mother about this she took me to task.

'You mustn't do that. Whatever you both intend, everyone will look on you as a married couple.'

When I told Tadashi Maekawa he replied, 'You mustn't live alone with him. Both you and he are so alike that if you live together it will do neither of you any good.'

Although he had said previously it was all right if one was not too young, when he heard that Yasuhiko wanted to live with me for some reason he was violently against it.

'Neither of you have much desire to live. If you get to discussing suicide together you'll both agree on a double suicide and then there'll be trouble.'

Having said this, he urged me if possible to stop seeing Yasuhiko Mafuji. I attributed this to jealousy.

A few days after this Tadashi Maekawa said as soon as he met me, 'Aya-chan! They're saying you're an awful schemer. I heard one of the young girls at church talking about you the other day.'

I could have replied 'She probably told you I was a flirt. Well, didn't you know that already? It's a bit late to sound surprised about such "awful" things now,' but I said nothing. I could see he had been deeply upset because he had heard the story from the girl he knew so well. Deep in my heart I simply wanted to go off with Yasuhiko Mafuji and live quietly in a town where no one knew us.

16

The whiteness of winter came. The snow lay deep on the earth. My own heart was as bleak as the winter.[11] I was miserable because of the gossip about me. But one night in bed as I gazed absentmindedly at the ceiling I saw one strand of a spider's web swaying. A stove was burning in the room, so there were probably air currents. The thread drifted softly from left to right, but because one end was firmly attached to the ceiling it stayed in the same place. As I watched it I thought, 'However much you hate this town and

[11] From early childhood Japanese develop a keen sensitivity to the moods of nature, endeavouring to harmonise their own lives with nature and so avoid conflict. There are numerous instances in this book.

flee to the back of beyond, in the end you can't budge an inch. You're tied by the tail.'

After that the idea of running away became amusing. However far I fled I could not escape my hatefulness, and when I realised I could never escape from myself it became meaningless to run away to some place where I was unknown.

I would like to assure you at this point that although I had had many men friends, I had never lost my head or surrendered myself completely to anyone. I was not aware of seeking male company through physical desire, but because I wanted to discuss life with them.[12] I think you will understand if I quote from a letter of mine at that time.

December 27th, 1950, from Ayako to Tadashi Maekawa:

Tadashi-san, I haven't picked up my pen to write idle reminiscences to you today.

The other night you said a girl at church warned you that I was a schemer and a horrible person. I want to write about this. I have shown you the poem,

> Listening to the rumour that I was a flirt
> I smiled without admitting it.

The poem said 'without admitting it', but I do admit my flirtatious nature. I admit that I am a flirt by nature, but I never consciously set out to seduce or deceive men to get money out of them. That was not what I wanted.

When men said they loved me I listened eagerly, seriously, with interest and longing, as a child listens to a fairy story, because for me the love of a man for a woman and a woman for a man was so important.

Do you know what I longed for so earnestly? I wanted

[12] She was looking for men for intellectual companionship in a culture where traditionally companionship was found only with those of one's own sex, and women belonged 'in the house' (see Author's Preface, The Beginning). Hence the criticism levelled at her, and her longing to be treated as a person in her own right.

to discover the one thing essential for living. I thought this thing I looked for must be connected with love.

'I love you. I will give my life for you.' What sort of woman does this apply to? It's no good asking 'What does "I love you" mean?' because for some people 'I love you' means 'I like you', for some it means 'I want you physically', and for others 'I want to marry you'. But the very meaning of the word 'marriage' is vague, so how can they say 'I love you' when they don't know what they mean by it?

Some people think my restlessness in life can be solved through marriage, through the embrace of a man, but this does not mean he would love me as a person.

Loving a 'woman', and loving Ayako or someone else as a person are different. I feel so restless because if there had been someone who had understood me even a little, and my longing for something I do not understand, he might have gazed at me and told me he loved me. But that person still hasn't appeared, although I have searched everywhere for someone to be with me and encourage me.

How many men there must be who don't realise that a woman has a spiritual nature. One is given lovely brooches, invitations to the cinema or tea house, and boring conversations. I have had glimpses into the hearts of one and another, and I have fled. I don't deny the term 'flirt'. If this is said of a woman without any particular beauty or wisdom or worth when she associated with men, it can't be helped.

I think it is strangely sad that I have had no physical relationship with any man; supposing instead that I had completely surrendered myself physically to someone, I could then have said, 'I have been faithful. I'm true to one man. I'm not a flirt.' Do you understand, Tadashi-san?

When I re-read this, it's a horrible letter. Are you thinking my flirtatious nature is due to the triviality of men? It isn't. I'm just a very bad woman.

Since rumours arise from malice and curiosity, the rumours about me must be lurid indeed, but my inherent

hatefulness is far worse than the spoken rumours. Nobody
knows about that. Be careful when you come near me,
Tadashi-san! If you follow the saying, 'A wise man will
flee from danger', run for your life and don't look back.
By so doing you will repay the kindness of the lady who
warned you about me. Here I shed a few tears — but only
a few. What are the tears of a flirt worth?

Good luck and a happy New Year! I'm going to post
this letter now and then I'm going to watch the crows
flocking over the Ushubetsu rubbish tip. I like the flocks
of black crows hunting over the snow-covered dump.

From the dangerous flirt, Ayako, to the virtuous Christian boy.

17

The New Year dawned. Surprisingly, Tadashi Maekawa and
I became even more friendly than we were before, and the
rumours he had heard from his girl friend only served to
draw us closer together after all.

At that time I used to visit Asahikawa Health Centre once
a week for pneumothorax therapy. Today, with the develop-
ment of streptomycin and plastic surgery, this treatment
may have disappeared, but at that time all tubercular
patients with cavities received it. A large needle was inserted
into the chest. A rubber tube was attached to this needle and
air was released into the pleural cavity. When the air entered
the cavity it compressed the lung and the infected part of the
lung collapsed.

Everyone remembers the first time this large needle was
inserted without any anaesthetic, though the needle itself
was not so painful in spite of its size. The pain came when
air first entered the chest. Even though one took a breath it
was too painful to speak. But after the first time the pain
of the air entering gradually decreased until before long
we felt so much better we looked forward eagerly to the
treatment.

But this does not mean that it was always safe. One patient was about to be discharged and on the day for treatment was called by the nurse and walked off cheerfully humming. He never came back. The instrument was able to measure the pressure in the thorax, but the doctor was careless. The air entered a vein and he died of an air embolism. We all feared the injection of air into a vein.

Moreover, the needle which was supposed only to enter the pleural cavity sometimes perforated the lung. Then, when the patient breathed, air leaked into the cavity, the lungs suddenly collapsed, the patient lost consciousness and soon died. This mishap occurred time and again. Those of us who received this treatment feared spontaneous pneumothorax as much as we feared an air embolism. I heard that this accident tended to happen when doctors, however experienced, were joking with patients and nurses. However rare the accident it was not impossible, so most people felt uneasy when undergoing such treatment.

One snowy day I went to the Health Centre for treatment as usual. When it was over, I was about to leave the room when suddenly everything went black. The nurse grabbed me and gently laid me down on a nearby couch. The doctor hurriedly took my pulse and in all it took no more than thirty seconds. Instantly I felt the dreaded mishap had occurred, and then I thought, 'Am I going to die? Well, there is nothing I can do about it'. The next thing I thought of was not my father and mother, but 'I must hand over the books for the TB Patients' Association'.

Two or three hours later I had fortunately returned to normal. It was neither spontaneous pneumothorax nor an air embolism. They called it 'shock'. But this incident was a valuable lesson to me, because I faced my last moments suddenly, without warning.

I had thought about dying before that, but I had not anticipated that death would overtake me suddenly against my will. I had never been very positive about living and had always been rather weak-willed. One night when I was nine, I had thought about death. Wondering why people die, I

could not get to sleep however much I tried, and I came to
the conclusion, 'Even if everybody else dies, I won't'.

After brooding about death from childhood, I had a sacri-
legious tenacity for living,[13] so I had always expected that
if I were suddenly overtaken by death I would face it in an
improper way. But when the moment came, unexpectedly I
was suitably resigned and could calmly say 'There's nothing
I can do about it. Am I going to die now? All right!' Needless to say, I bore the doctor no resentment whatsoever. The
strangest thing of all was that instead of my father, mother,
family and friends, I thought first of handing over the register for the Patients' Association, for which I received a
mere pound a month, and this was not my career but a part-
time job. I had not usually thought it so important. Why
then did it come to mind at that moment? I had not even
wished for a glimpse of Tadashi Maekawa whom I had
known so well.

This experience taught me firstly that, although men fear
death, if they suddenly meet it head on, to their surprise they
may quietly accept it. And secondly, we can live in ignorance
of ourselves. Whatever we imagine we will do when we die,
we may still have an entirely unforeseen reaction. After this
I may face death quite differently.

Men often measure others by the way they die, but I question whether one should judge people by the way they face
sudden death. If I had died then, they would have reported
that I did so with a proper spirit, but I think that when my
time really comes, I will probably resist it.

Naturally this scare influenced my life in various ways.
That night by the sea when I had pleaded to die, I could not,
but now when I had begun to want to live, I did not know
how soon death would visit me. I felt this unwelcome threat
very deeply. Was my will to be trampled heedlessly under
foot? Yet when I reflected on this I could not help feeling
that there must be a Will at work in the world even stronger

[13] From childhood the Japanese are encouraged to prepare themselves
to accept death with courage and tranquility of mind. How one faces
death is an important feature in life.

and greater than our own, intervening in our ordinary, everyday lives.

Let me explain. We make a rough plan today to do the laundry, read a book, go shopping in the town. But just as we are ready to hang the clothes out it begins to rain, in the midst of reading the book we begin to get a stomach-ache, and just as we are setting off for the town a visitor arrives. You can never organise your life as you want to.

It had happened many times in my twenty-eight years of life. The most obvious instance was the day Ichiro Nishinaka's engagement gift arrived, and I was taken ill and soon had tuberculosis, and all the wedding plans were thrown into confusion.

Since our own grip on things is so feeble, what sort of Person is it who overrules our human plans? Before long I realised that of course this 'Person' was the Supreme Being, God.

18

One day in March when the melting snow was dripping steadily from the eaves, a card arrived from Yasuhiko Mafuji, with rows of small uneven characters scattered across it.

> Ayako-san, how are you? I only have one post card to hand here. Tomorrow I am having thoracic surgery. I thought I would not tell anyone beforehand, but on seeing this postcard I picked up my pen and decided just to tell you.

The wording was simple enough, but the content was serious. By 'thoracic surgery' he meant that several ribs would be removed. Though it was no more dangerous than that, it was a big operation. I showed the card to Tadashi Maekawa who happened to be visiting me when it arrived. He read it through and sprang to his feet.

'Let's go immediately. Maybe there's something we can do to help, and anyway it will encourage him to have someone near.'

'But I've got a temperature today.' He stopped me with a look of disgust.

'Mafuji-san's operation is a matter of life and death!'

Yasuhiko Mafuji had no mother, and it was certainly pitiful not to have the one you needed most with you when you faced surgery. However, what concerned me was that he had sent his only postcard to me, for he had plenty of friends, both male and female. To be honest, the fact was by no means unpleasant. Although Tadashi Maekawa had earlier urged me to sever my friendship with Yasuhiko Mafuji, he himself sent him poems and magazines and postcards. For some reason Mafuji had never done anything in return. I had the impression he read them indifferently and threw them away. So I hesitated, feeling that there was no need for Tadashi Maekawa to get involved in Yasuhiko Mafuji's operation.

We went to the hospital and found that the necessary preparations had not yet been made. For example, although oiled paper for lying on and a feeding cup were essential for surgical patients, nothing was ready. Tadashi Maekawa, with the methodical concern of a medical student, wrote down what was required and gave the list to his eldest sister. Then, feeling a large ward of eight people might be trying, he arranged with the doctor for him to be moved to a double room.

The operation was the next day. Tadashi Maekawa and I went once more to the hospital. Mafuji received his basal anaesthetic and was wheeled off on a trolley to the theatre. While we waited for the operation to finish I bought some caramels at the shop and offered one to the weary-looking Tadashi Maekawa.

'How about a caramel?'

He shook his head indignantly. 'Mafuji is in the theatre, in the middle of his operation. A caramel would stick in my throat.'

His words struck me. Mafuji was not always kind to Tadashi Maekawa. Indeed, as I have said, he could be quite cold. I felt that Tadashi Maekawa's genuine concern for Mafuji's operation was quite remarkable. I opened the box of caramels and ate them by myself.

19

Yasuhiko Mafuji's operation was successful and little by little he regained his strength. Tadashi Maekawa visited him even more than I did, and occasionally we went to see him together, whereupon Mafuji remarked, 'The patients and nurses are wondering whether you're brother and sister'. Our relationship did not strike even casual observers as romantic.

I had large eyes with double eyelids, Tadashi Maekawa had narrow eyes with single eyelids,[14] and although we did not look alike I was glad that we seemed to have something in common. Nihilistic as I thought myself, I was glad of any sign of progress, however small, which made me more like him.

One day Tadashi Maekawa bought me a large notebook. 'Let's write down our comments on what we read!' he said. He seemed delighted when he could help me make even a little progress, and one by one he brought me Gheorghiu's *25 o'clock*, Rilke's *Memoirs of Marte* and Yuriko and Kenji Miyamoto's *Twelve Years' Correspondence* and made me write down my comments.

Most men and women would not spend their time together on such 'homework', but I enjoyed it. I felt like Rilke, who said, 'There is no lovelier relationship than that of a young girl who wants to learn and a young man who wants to teach.' We wanted to be like that, so together we earnestly read the Bible, studied English and read poetry. Tadashi-san had begun writing poetry in 1946 and was a contributor to

[14] The Japanese describe 'oriental' eyes as having single eyelids and 'western' eyes as having double eyelids.

Araragi.[15] Having only just begun to write poetry myself I could not fully grasp the skill of his poems, but I was moved by the deep humanity of this one:

> Walking together through a grove of trees in the park,
> I had the illusion that we were lovers.
> I walked along the dark road with an innocent girl,
> Wondering what would happen if I suddenly embraced her.

The girl he wrote about was not me. She was the one who had told him previously that I was a schemer. When he showed it to me he said he had written it at a church conference, and I was astonished.

'Well! Who would have thought someone as sober-minded as you would think of things like that!'

'Aya-chan, you may read novels, but you still don't know the first thing about men. When I ask you, you cheerfully come with me to a deserted place like Shunkodai, but, after all, I am a man and you really ought to be more careful.'

'But I'm not the least bit afraid of men. They know what's right and what's wrong, so I don't expect them to be reckless and do anything they shouldn't.'

'Exactly! That's just why I don't know what to do with you. You're like a child who can't see whether something is dangerous or not. Kikuchi Kan[16] said only the *geisha* really know men, but I wish you would learn a little more about them.' Gravely he warned me not to trust them.

This was new to me. Each of my friends had behaved like a gentleman and no one had ever before suggested that men in general could not be trusted.

Tadashi Maekawa continued, 'Take me. I may appear to be well-behaved, but inside my heart is a whirl of evil thoughts.'

Inwardly I decided once more that this sort of person was

[15] See note on page 52.
[16] A well-known Japanese writer and playwright, 1888–1948.

good and could be trusted, yet time and again in one way or another he seemed to be trying to prevent me trusting him, saying,

'I have dreams I can't repeat to anyone, but even so this is quite a good poem:

> As I briefly kissed her lips,
> I awoke, breathing heavily.

'Aya-chan, you're a woman, and being a woman you need to know what sort of person your life partner really is. It's because people imagine men to be pure and marry this imaginary vision that there are so many unhappy marriages.'

So he would try to teach me. Looking back now, I realise he may have hated to see himself idealised; but more than that, I believe he was thinking about my future. Knowing his own life would be brief, he was concerned lest in my ignorance I made a poor marriage. Another of his poems had the same implications:

> When I cautiously kept my distance in friendship,
> One after another the girls left me.

He was also deeply concerned with the problem of peace. He greatly respected the sincerity of a member of the Asahikawa Communist Party, and used to attend the Communist peace gatherings. In his enthusiasm he was drawn for a while towards the Party, as the following poem shows:

> Because I cannot make the decision to go underground
> I am silent when you urge me to join the Party.

If he had been urged to become a member he must have shown himself fairly sympathetic, but he said he lacked the strength of the true Communist who held to his convictions even when these were illegal. Yet he seemed to feel that peace itself must be preserved at all costs and often spoke to

me about it. On one occasion when we were discussing the
problem of peace together on the river-bank, two or three
passing fellows made some facetious comments.

'To other people we must look like a pair of lovers having
a heart to heart! It's part of the tragedy of life that a young
couple like us have to sit on a lovely river-bank discussing
peace, of all things.' And he laughed.

It was then that I began to think seriously about the
problem of peace. There must have been millions of young
lovers in the world. If they were content to talk only about
their feelings, that was all right. But how tragic it would be
if they had to say, 'How soon is the next war going to be?
When it comes, you'll be in the front lines, won't you?'

I remarked, 'Who wants a car or a big house! One room
is enough, if only we and our families can live without
worrying about war.'

In his longing for peace he wrote several poems along
these lines:

Is prayer the only way to peace?
We Christians have neither organisation nor force.

With growing uneasiness the young are afraid
When they tell of their teachers joining the Party.

Now of all times I do not want to compromise as a
   Christian.
The foreign news proclaims the misery of atomic war.

When I wondered whether the desire for peace would
   ever be fulfilled
The weather-vane changed direction.

Now it is over, the group boast of their splendid
   isolation
When they were passive, not encouraging the war.

Another time he told me how to read the newspaper.

'Aya-chan! Big headlines don't mean important articles, because sometimes the really significant things are in small print, in two or three lines in a corner of the page. You must keep your eyes open and read thoughtfully, asking what it means in today's world.'

Later I found this truth endorsed over and over again, and he himself wrote,

> One fearfully tried to draw conclusions
> From the brief articles from abroad.

He was thirty-one at that time, but still a convalescent medical student of Hokudai University, so it was natural for him to write:

> The revolution is spreading in China,
> I am deeply impressed with the students who take part
> in it.

> The students surround the notice opposing conscription.
> One of them is cradling a bowl of crocuses.

I particularly like the second poem, feeling that the sincere youthfulness of those young students opposed to conscription was symbolised by the one who protected the crocuses from harm. Even today I would not hesitate to offer this poem as exemplary for Youth Day.

20

My own poems, while clumsy, began to change considerably. When I began writing, many of them had been nihilistic:

> The thought has often come that I could die
> If I took twice the maximum dose —
> But the day has come to an end.

When I am utterly disgusted with myself,
The dark and murky clouds overwhelm me.

I shake the thermometer down;
I am alive but accomplishing nothing.

Tonight I envy the beggars
Lying on the Post Office bench.

Somewhere along the way, that sort of poem changed:

I read the Vacancies column in The Housewives'
  Friend.
Is there a way for me to make a living, sick as I am?

I change into a nightdress smelling of formalin
And I am coming to accept it.

Meanwhile Tadashi Maekawa had to go to the Hokudai
University Hospital for investigation. I was uneasy about it
but not on account of his health. It was because the first girl
he ever fell in love with, lived in Sapporo. She was the
daughter of his landlord and four years older than he. Although he described her as his first love he had kept it to
himself and she married, knowing nothing of it.

In actual fact, as she was very intelligent she may have
been aware of his feelings, but if so she feigned ignorance
and handled the matter tactfully. When he told me about
this he said gratefully, 'It was a good thing. When you are
young there are times when it is all right to fall in love, but
better not to be loved in return.'

This was when he sensed the dangerous situation between
myself and Yasuhiko Mafuji, who was seven years younger.

At all events, when I heard he was going to Sapporo I felt
instinctively that he would bump into her again. I sometimes
had a prophetic sense of what was going to happen that day.
Especially when I was in hospital, lying with every nerve
taut, I could sometimes tell what was being made in the
kitchen a hundred yards away.

During the brief week he spent in Sapporo he sent me twenty-eight postcards.

I have just arrived at Sapporo station. It is much warmer than Asahikawa. I'm off to the hospital now, but first I am dropping you a quick note. Take care of yourself while I am away.

The contents were as simple as that, but sometimes from the waiting-room, sometimes from the canteen, and sometimes from a nearby bookshop, he assiduously sent me news. The things he had eaten, the people he had met, what Sapporo was like, he reported everything from beginning to end, just as if he were trying to give me the feeling that I was there with him.

Before long I found in his cards what I had feared.

Today it is mild in Sapporo, but the crisp snow is trying underfoot. I met someone unexpectedly today. It was Aki. The red beret and lipstick were the same. Seeing her walking along with a five-year-old boy, her head inclined to one side a little, it was just like seven years ago. She did not seem to have noticed me, so I passed without speaking.

Realising that my intuition had come true, I read the card over and over, wondering if his feelings about her were concealed between the lines. Then I decided he still loved her after all. If he didn't love her there was no reason to hesitate, when they had lived under one roof for several years. It would have been natural to mention her name without thinking.

It was extraordinary to recall that her beret and even her lipstick were the same as seven years previously. To see her in such circumstances and yet to pass by in that way must mean that, whatever he said, he still loved her.

His week in Sapporo soon ended and he returned to Asahikawa. As soon as we met I remarked, 'So you met her.'

That was all I had to say in spite of the pleasure of receiving twenty-eight postcards full of news. It was then that I became vividly aware that I loved Tadashi Maekawa. Though I had associated with him as a teacher and a friend until now, suddenly my heart turned towards him.

'Yes, I met her,' he remarked with a smile and asked, 'Is anything the matter?'

I said nothing. Meeting her again after seven years, he would remember things he thought he had forgotten.

'Aya-chan!'

Raising my head at his voice, I found myself looking into his eyes. Those eyes eloquently revealed his feelings.

'Why didn't you speak to her?' As I spoke emotion flooded his face.

'Aya-chan, it's not just her. There are lots of women I don't speak to' — and so saying he took my hand for the first time. From that day we were no longer simply friends.

For the first time in my life I wrote love poems:

> For two years I have been guided and scolded
> And suddenly I am deeply in love.

> In a room filled with the smell of smouldering hair,
> I cannot bear to think about you.[17]

By and by the snow melted and spring came to Hokkaido. It was May and suddenly the cherry was in flower. May in Asahikawa is beautiful. Sometimes we went together to Shunkodai Hill, the place where he had struck his foot with a stone for my sake. Early one morning he said,

'Aya-chan, I thought we'd celebrate your birthday today.'

My birthday was April 25th and I had received a book. At the confectioner's he bought four cakes and I went up the hill, assuming he had bought them for me as a gift because I liked sweet things.

Overlooking the town where we lived, dim in a purple

---

[17] Hair was the symbol of womanhood. A few strands had been thrown into a charcoal brazier.

haze of smoke, we talked as usual about novels and poetry. In the nearby pasture a herd of cows slowly cropped the grass as they went past. The cowherd, about eleven years of age, was playing a grass flute. He passed us without so much as a glance and then the two of us were alone again on the hill. Not a single house was there and the hill seemed remote and quiet.

That day we kissed each other for the first time and he said, 'That's to celebrate your birthday.'

I was taken by surprise. 'My birthday present? It's a lovely gift.'

Quietly he knelt on the fresh grass and prayed for us both. 'Heavenly Father, you know that we are both ill, but please help us to spend our brief lives truly and purposefully. Please help us to be faithful to you and each other until the last day.'

We suddenly found ourselves in tears. I was crying because I was deeply touched with the reality of his love, but I wonder if he was crying for me, knowing his own life would be brief, and wondering how long it would be before I was left alone. I can still hear him saying, 'Let's live with all we have.'

> Both of us ill, wondering how long our happiness will last,
> We kiss and weep.
>
> *Ayako*

> My heart sings like a flute as I hold you close;
> Sadness sweeps over me.
>
> *Tadashi*

21

As the happy days passed with Tadashi Maekawa, I was once more assailed by an indefinable sense of uneasiness, for my present contentment depended entirely upon Tadashi Maekawa's existence.

To be sure he was kind and conversation was plentiful, and as lovers we were happy together. We did not kiss when we met, for he preferred stoic discipline! Our relationship was as pure and fresh as a bracing breeze. But the more I trusted him for his attitude, the more I wondered uneasily whether the tranquillity I had found was what I had been looking for.

My happiness lay in the existence of one man, Tadashi Maekawa. If this were so, if ever he left me or died, the foundation of my present happiness would collapse. At this point I was very self-centred. Momentary happiness made me insecure. I wanted a permanent happiness that would last for ever. I was afraid, and I became increasingly conscious of this fear.

Under his influence I continued to read as many books as possible, and *The Voice of the Ocean* was one of these. It was a bestseller at that time and is read by students even today. It is the letters and diaries of student soldiers who died in action. When I finished reading it, I felt it was one book you could not say you had finished reading. I was impressed by it yet reading alone was not enough. It was a book which demanded a response in the life of the reader.

In *The Voice of the Ocean* almost all these young men at least criticised the war, but they all took part in the war they denounced and not one of them condemned it absolutely. Not one was strong enough to risk his life by refusing to take part in it. So I felt apprehensive and lonely as I realised that ultimately even education had its limitations. And the book seemed even more tragic as I bitterly regretted those young lives swept into oblivion.

I began to see that real peace would not come through mere pacifism. In view of the value of human life, something was necessary to deny absolutely the cruel nature within every man, and I could find no other name for this except 'God'. But I could not accept Christianity. Christianity existed in warring America, England, France and Germany. Had not Christ lacked the power to end the war? If that were so, then religion was as powerless as learning. So despair swept over me. The world had lost the true God, and I was dissatisfied with a church which had apparently failed to realise this.

Moreover, however much people read *The Voice of the Ocean* and grieved over it, the war could still happen again. You did not have to read this book to learn that because of war most Japanese people had lost friends and relatives, their homes had been burnt and their own fate drastically changed. To a greater or lesser extent most of the population had become victims of the war. Because of wartime food shortages we tubercular patients had had to endure months of illness when it need never have happened. But in spite of all this we do not resolve that there will never be another. Men are stupid and dim-witted. If an individual murdered or burnt houses, he would never be forgiven, but we say with our lips, 'We renounce war. We paid dearly for it', and there is no violent indignation in our hearts.

I became afraid when I realised the dullness and indifference within myself. Unless there were first a real and burning desire for peace in the heart of each person, it would remain an insoluble problem. The purer the motives of those young *Voice of the Ocean* students, the more I could not help feeling that, to eliminate war, someone called 'God' was necessary. At all events, one thing was certain. This book had marked a great step forward in my journey to faith.

22

I began to search in earnest and also to take care of myself more seriously. One day Tadashi Maekawa suggested,

'Aya-chan, why don't we both go to Hokudai University Hospital for a medical check-up?'

For his family the cost of a check-up in Sapporo would not be too great a burden, but for my family, with my brothers still in middle school and high school, it was by no means easy. I went immediately to the wholesale shop and collected a stock of men's and women's socks, and walked around the sanatorium and from door to door in the town selling them. It was barely the middle of June, a beautiful time of year filled with the scent of lilac, but I was fortunate if one house in ten bought from me, and I could not stand up to it physically. Then I went to sell them at the bank where my friend worked.

'Just wait a moment,' she exclaimed cheerfully. 'Have a rest here while I sell them for you.' And she went round her colleagues and had sold everything in less than no time. I am still grateful for what she did for me, even today.

Gradually the money accumulated until the morning came when the two of us left for Sapporo. When I reached the station, I found Tadashi carrying a rucksack on his back. I was astonished, because at that time no one wearing a suit would carry a rucksack. But when I asked, 'Why didn't you bring a suitcase?', he answered with a smile, 'Because I wanted both hands free to carry your luggage', and he picked mine up.

I was embarrassed. He would not enjoy carrying a rucksack on his back when wearing a suit, but he had thought of me rather than himself. The thought came to me, 'Our journey together through life will be like this. If he marries me it will be like carrying that rucksack all his life and I'll be nothing but a burden to him.'

He was to stay with a friend and I was to stay with my mother's aunt. He took my luggage to the door and left.

Suddenly I realised I was still holding his green *furoshiki*.[18] I had carried it simply because it was light, containing only his diary. I did not know his address to return it. It would probably be all right to give it back the following morning at the hospital, but a diligent writer such as he would certainly want to write in it that night. So I felt rather troubled about it. At bedtime I lay down with the *furoshiki* by my pillow. Suddenly the thought came to me, 'Try reading a bit'.

Of course I was strongly against prying into people's letters or even postcards. But, understandably, I was very

[18] Traditionally anything carried outside the house is wrapped in an attractive square cloth of appropriate size, called a *furoshiki*.

curious and as it was my fiancé's diary, it was natural to want to read it. However, when he gave it to me he had not said I could. Everyone has things they don't want others to know about and if I had read it without permission I would have betrayed him. I did not want to slight him by reading it, so in the end I went to sleep leaving the diary by my pillow untouched.

The next day when we met at the hospital I handed it over saying, 'I wanted to read it but I didn't,' and with an easy smile he answered, 'You could have read it.'

I seem to remember Hokudai University Hospital was then a two-storey concrete building. The long corridors we patients had to pass through from one department to another felt more like three blocks. From the windows we could see the walls of the wards covered with soft green ivy. Walking with him along those corridors I felt like crying, for in all the departments his former fellow-students were in white coats briskly examining patients.

'It's nothing much. You'll soon be better,' they assured him. What did he feel deep down, when he was past thirty and still an undergraduate with no idea when he would be better? I could not hold back my tears. It was especially hard when he went for a chest X-ray. I do not know whether it was a professor or lecturer who was teaching a group of students, but when he saw Tadashi Maekawa he saw him only as good teaching material. He got him to strip to the waist and continued his lecture. In his gentle way Tadashi-san stood stripped in front of the students, smiling, a model visual aid. Of course they could not be expected to know he was senior to them.

When I suggested, with something akin to anger, that it would have been better if I had stood there instead of him, he answered in his usual reasonable way.

'Aya-chan, every man is given his own way to walk. Weren't you even a little glad to see my friends had become fully-fledged doctors?' He had diagnosed my feelings correctly and comforted me by saying, 'When I entered the university I expected to become a doctor a few years later. I would have had an income of so much; I didn't anticipate lacking food, and was proud of a medical career. But because I trust in God I believe that the way given to me is the best one and I can give thanks for it. There is no need to be sad about it, Aya-chan.'

Sensing in his words the strength and beauty of one who was ready to sacrifice his life, I nodded in silence.

When the first day's tests were finished we walked all over the medical school. He took me to the dissecting room and the mortuary attached to it and so on. Thinking that he must certainly have many memories connected with every corner of this musty place, I could not but feel sorry for him.

When we went out into the grounds, the green of the grass was so fresh. The huge elm trees, hundreds of years old, were as lovely as a grove of trees in a park. White-coated doctors and nurses and students walked beneath them, chatting cheerfully. Inadvertently I remarked, 'Those people are lucky, aren't they?'

He became serious and replied, 'I wouldn't say that.'

'Why?'

'Because you cannot say people are happy just because they appear happy. See that nurse walking past the lilacs? Maybe discussions about her marriage were broken off yesterday. The student behind her may have a sick father at home and be afraid in case he can't finish his studies.'

'Well, well! You've a vivid imagination!'

'So ultimately we shouldn't envy people in their "happiness". You could say I'm perfectly happy just walking across the grass together with you.' There was not a shadow on his face.

We spent the next day also at the hospital, and when the tests were over we dined in the canteen and then together we visited the Sapporo shrine on the evening of the shrine festival. That evening Tadashi-san bought me Tatsuo Hori's book *Naoko* at a second-hand bookshop, and the writing is still on the flyleaf today:

To Aya-chan.

We walked through Sapporo to your lodging on the eve of the shrine festival. Then we set off together again to see Sapporo by night and stopped at a second-hand bookshop. In between customers and gossiping and smoking, the kimono-clad shopkeeper searched for a book we asked for. Both the author and the heroine Naoko had tuberculosis, this wonderful tuberculosis which brought you and me to the university hospital for treatment.

While drinking *mocha* coffee in a Sapporo coffee shop,

Tadashi.

The following day, to avoid the Sapporo festival, we boarded the train for Asahikawa. On the return trip he sat beside me writing innumerable postcards. He wrote immediately to thank the people with whom he had stayed in Sapporo, and his friends. After a trip he always wrote notes of thanks on the return journey, and when I admired him for being so methodical he answered with a smile, 'I probably ought to write after I got home, because it isn't really true to say "I have returned home safely, thank you" '.

The diagnoses at the Sapporo hospital revealed nothing very extraordinary about either of us, which meant that there was no cause for joy in his diagnosis. They could not operate and chloromycetin had little effect. When the time came he would die.

In my case, there was hope of a cure with artificial pneumothorax treatment, though the low fever and loss of weight continued in spite of the fairly good X-ray.

The day after we reached home a postcard promptly arrived from him. He had written it sitting next to me on the train! There was this humorous side of him too, a humour which involved paying great attention to the person he had been with for three days. I think this card included an impromptu poem, which used the sound of the train, 'gotton-gotton', in several places. Today when I recall our journey there is one thing I am secretly proud of — that, far from being at all like the present popular pre-wedding trip, on

ours we did not exchange a single kiss. Probably he was all
the more discreet because we were travelling. He seemed to
have an iron will and a masculine decisiveness in judgment.
Something of it is revealed in this letter:

> I received your card this afternoon. You probably
> wrote it last night. In it you remarked that so much had
> been erased in my recent card I clearly hadn't told you all
> I was thinking about. Actually I wrote a little about my
> feelings for you and then changed my mind and crossed it
> out. At present it would mean nothing to you and, what
> is more, our circumstances do not make it necessary.

As far as possible he did not use affectionate words as he
did not like an emotionally-charged atmosphere. Moreover,
I think we both needed firm discipline more than endear-
ments. If a man and woman are not careful in their relationship, their lives become slovenly and idle. In his cards from
that period the word 'diligence' aptly occurs. I think we both
wanted to spur each other on in the right sense.

September came, the time when Yasuhiko Mafuji finally
returned to Sapporo. The surgery had been completely
successful and he had recovered so well he could go back to
University.

The day before he left he came to my house to say goodbye. Mafuji did not bother to visit Tadashi Maekawa before
leaving, but the next day in thick fog Tadashi went to the
station to see him off.

23

That autumn I became even thinner, my eyes were dull, my
cheeks flushed with the fever. The doctor looked at the
chest X-rays, found no cause for the fever and said it was
probably due to my highly-strung temperament.

From that time I gradually lost faith in doctors. The
human body is a delicate and complicated thing. I did not

see why, when my temperature persisted at 37·4°C (99°F)
and I gradually grew thinner, the doctor should merely look
at the X-ray and inform me that I was highly strung.
Weren't doctors scientists? A scientist was someone who
had to investigate the unknown, but this doctor had not
enquired further. He simply picked on my lack of exercise
and advised working. From the beginning, when my coughing showed signs of blood, he had taken no notice, remark-
ing, 'Isn't it from the nose? If you cough hard it sometimes
makes the throat bleed.'

At such times it is miserable to be ill. If you know the
cause of the temperature and loss of weight you can treat it
and bear with some suffering, but to become weaker, with
the doctor insisting that nothing is wrong, is far more dis-
tressing. I felt as if the life within me was being devoured, to
mock me just as I had begun to take it seriously. However
much science had progressed, it seemed unable to discover
what was wrong with me. What sort of science was that?

I felt I was living in a terribly unenlightened age and began
to think frequently that mankind knew nothing. In the long
course of history, I felt, this present age of ours was more
like an ancient era[19]. It seemed strange to extol it and glorify
science. At that point I found the words in the Bible, 'If a
man thinks he knows something, he does not yet know what
he ought to know', and they struck a deep chord within me.
'What he ought to know' — could this mean God, I wondered. I was reading my Bible quite a lot but was still
unconvinced.

When I talked to friends about God, I was often told,
'There can't be a God. In today's scientific, progressive
world, if something cannot be proved it is the same as not
existing.'

Then suddenly I wanted to laugh. Has this world made so
much scientific progress? Are men as clever as that! They
think they understand every single thing when they do not
even understand their own bodies. Science is no more than

---

[19] The Buddhist view of history is cyclic rather than linear.

man's inventions. Even if a plane flies, the atom bomb is invented, and a rocket sent to the moon, how much does he understand of the infinite universe? I argued.

'All right. Since we cannot prove God's existence, if you say there is no God, I want you to prove that.'

Then most of my friends would pause and scratch their heads. If there was no scientific proof that God did not exist, then it was unscientific to say He did not. They denied His existence, saying it was unscientific to say there was a God when there was not, but they did not recognise that this was the same as acknowledging His existence.

At the same time we discussed whether man was big or small. Sometimes man seemed absurdly small and we could imagine ourselves as a virus living in a giant cell. The space between cell and cell was as great as that between star and star. It was fun to think of the giant cell as the world with buildings on it and trains crossing it, though from the giant's point of view the existence of millions of men would make no impression. But though it might be fun to imagine something like that, it was no comfort to me when in actual fact I was living and suffering. The problem still lay in my own human heart.

When I read Pascal's *Pensées* I was interested in his 'wager'. 'Well, if I wager there is a God, I can believe in Him and live a life of fulfilment and hope. But if I live as if there is no God, being human I may become slovenly, indifferent, taken up with worthless pleasures and waste my whole life; and if God does exist, ultimately how can I come before Him when I have never once believed in Him?'

I kept on thinking about that. Did God exist or did He not? Which of these was true? Either it was a lie to say casually that He existed or a lie to say that He did not. This was the crux of the matter — did He exist or didn't He?

Some people might say it was better to spend one's life without worrying about this God, wondering whether He existed or not. But this did not satisfy me, because even if men did not know the answer, either He did or He didn't. Having got myself involved in this problem, I could not give up without an answer, and though I thought I ought to take a chance on there being a God, I could not bring myself to do this.

By now I was growing increasingly thinner and at Tadashi Maekawa's suggestion I entered hospital in Asahikawa again. It was just after October 20th, 1952, when the first snow was expected.

Tadashi Maekawa came to visit me daily. It was one and a half miles from his home to the hospital, and even by bicycle this was no small effort for someone as sick as he. On the evening of November 2nd he visited me and remarked as he left, 'I may bring you some red rice[20] tomorrow evening, but I won't promise, so don't count on it.'

The following evening he arrived at the hospital drenched by the rain, carrying a nest of lacquered boxes. Putting them down, he returned home immediately, saying that he had not had his evening meal.

Later his friend commented, 'When I went to visit Tadashi-san recently he was quite restless. Then he asked his mother for something and disappeared with a nest of boxes saying he would soon be back. When I asked his mother she said that he had taken them to you. So he walked out on me! He's quite extraordinary!'

He was a young man and always respected Maekawa. When I heard of this incident it made me think again about promises. Tadashi Maekawa, far from making easy promises, never made a promise in the first place. The Bible says, 'Do not swear but let your Yes mean Yes and your No mean No.' He knew how changeable man is and, moreover, man does not know what will happen tomorrow, so when most people would have said 'I'll bring you red rice tomorrow', he reminded me 'I'm not promising' as he left. But in spite of all this he came. He kept a friend waiting and made the three-mile round trip in wind and driving rain. What a deep and faithful love that revealed! It also taught me that a really genuine person does not make promises lightly.

[20] Rice mixed with red beans

24

My ward was a large room with eight beds. Some of the people were up and about, but others were confined to bed all the time. There were various patients with tuberculosis, diabetes, chest abscesses, peritonitis, and spinal TB. There was one teenage girl among them. She still wore the bobbed hair of a schoolgirl but there was something morose about her.

One day her teacher came to see her. The teacher was not a person of many words but the girl was terribly taciturn. I could hear her answering Yes and No, but that was all she had to say. Being in the next bed I could really sympathise with that teacher!

A few days later, for some reason or other, I was telling the others in the room about the tragic suicide of a sick friend. Everyone was instantly silent, exchanging embarrassed glances. I had not known that the high school girl had attempted suicide. She had taken sleeping pills and had been unconscious for three days and nights. Fortunately because her heart was strong she was saved, but as the medicine had affected her stomach she was still in hospital.

I had thought her a gastric case. When the other patients told me about her in private, however, I had a fresh feeling of kinship with her, for I too had once tried to take my life and failed.

Probably she also sensed a bond between us. I did not ask her about her attempted suicide because the wound was too recent, but as I watched her carefully I could see that she was not regaining her composure. She changed her clothes several times a day, but on the other hand she would spend half the day sitting vacantly on her bed, her face unwashed, her hair uncombed, gazing blankly into space. I sensed intuitively that if she continued to neglect herself like this she would certainly choose death a second time.

Again and again I said to myself, 'Don't let her die!' And

then I was amazed at myself. Previously if someone wanted to die I would acquiesce silently, thinking, 'Let them die then'. As I myself had no purpose in living it had seemed better to let people die if that was what they wanted. But now I was distressed and worried for the life of a girl I hardly knew.

One day I decided to speak to her frankly. She was sitting listlessly on a chair by my bed. It was the end of November, the days were cold and the snow was falling and melting continually.

'Rië-chan, why did you want to die?' For a moment her eyes flickered and then her face went blank again.

'So you've heard about it, Hotta-san?'

'Yes, I've heard about it, and I don't like to see you sitting there in silence looking as if you'll do it again.'

She hung her head.

'You know, you're conceited, Rië-chan. How can you know at sixteen or seventeen whether life's worth living or not? What made you think of a futile thing like dying?'

I spoke bluntly. I felt I was talking to myself. When I mentioned the word 'conceited' she broke into a smile. She had a fearfully vacant look at times, but sometimes her eyes brightened and with her supple body she seemed curiously like a lovable cat rubbing itself against people's legs.

Gradually she opened up to me, until one day she told me why she had resolved to commit suicide.

'There was a Japanese language teacher at the middle school I went to in the country. He got on so well with us that I felt he would understand everything. I thought he would listen to my problems.'

Her parents had a large shop in the town.

'What were these problems?'

At such times I always spoke briskly. I still do. It is one of my weak points, that when someone discloses their deep distress, instead of nodding in agreement as a friend I speak as if I reject them. But people who know me realise that it only happens when I am deeply moved. Because I am deeply moved I cannot give way to my feelings, so I speak harshly.

In spite of her youth her acute sensitivity enabled her to understand immediately.

'I was distressed because mankind seemed as worthless as flotsam drifting on the open sea. I wrote this down and sent it to this teacher. The next thing I knew, he seemed to be taking it as a love letter. And then, instead of simply not replying, he circulated the story among the other teachers.'

I too had been a teacher. Merely by hearing her story I could gauge how deeply wounded she had been. That teacher might talk as if he understood his pupils, but he was out of his depth with this precocious child's questions. He could not understand the genuine apprehension of a person who begins to have doubts about life. Moreover, he had accepted her trust in him as her teacher far too lightly. He did not realise what a solemn thing it is to be trusted.

I listened to her story with great indignation. Even when she later went on to Asahikawa High School, this distrust of the teacher, once implanted, could not be removed. And as if this were not enough, the girl developed a deep-rooted distrust of all adults and gradually grew weary of living.

'Hotta-san, I drank that medicine on August 20th, my birthday, and I burnt all my notebooks and photos up to that point. I did not want to leave any evidence that I had ever existed.'

'What about your last wishes?'

'I wrote nothing.'

And so she revealed to me what she had disclosed to no one else — the reason for her suicide. While she was weary of life, the real cause was that middle school teacher.

To an adult this may seem a trifling story but it is an extraordinary thing for a person to choose her own birthday as the day on which to die. I could not help sympathising with such deep distress, and then because I had been a teacher I began to feel that I must bear some responsibility for her too.

Even after the snow came, Tadashi Maekawa continued to visit me as usual. He always arrived smiling, wearing a ski hat and white face mask. The atmosphere of the ward was never cheerful. There was an air of something like despair among the women patients and they would join in singing bawdy songs such as I had never in my life heard before. When boy friends came to visit them they would get into bed together in broad daylight, and the nurses took no notice.

But gradually the atmosphere changed. It was getting near Christmas and all the wards were busy putting up decorations. Christmas trees appeared from somewhere or other, and every room worked hard. Our room alone for some reason or other remained in low spirits. When everyone began to say, 'Hotta-san why don't you decorate the room for us?' I mentioned what I had been turning over in my mind for some days.

'The other rooms have all been decorating Christmas trees, but Christmas isn't just decorating a tree. Why don't we celebrate Christmas in a different way? We could ask a pastor to tell us about Christ.'

I expected an awkward moment when everyone would reject the suggestion. It may seem strange that I should have wanted to invite the pastor when I was still not a believer, but I really wanted to get Rië-chan to face up to life. This seemed the only way. As for the other people in the room, not one of them seemed to have any hope, and that was true of me also.

When they heard my suggestion, their faces, and those in the other rooms of my ward, lit up. They decided to put the suggestion into effect immediately, and not only that, but someone suggested the invitation should be sent from the whole ward. I was dumbfounded. But I discovered the reason before long. It was Tadashi Maekawa.

25

I was surprised by their enthusiasm because I had not so far discussed religion with the other patients in my room. I felt ashamed at having assumed beforehand that they would not

want to listen to a straight talk. It was a mere two months
since I entered hospital and, for all their haziness, they were
showing this goodwill towards Christianity. It was not without reason.

Tadashi Maekawa came to visit me daily. When he could
not come he sent a letter. This alone was enough to impress
the other patients with his faithfulness. If a wife was sick for
a year, the question of divorce usually came up. I don't know
how many wives wept because of that. And even if divorce
were not discussed, the husband virtually gave up visiting her.

Boy friends were no different. There were two girls in the
room whose boy friends had dropped them as soon as they
became ill. So Tadashi Maekawa's faithfulness did much in
restoring hope to these women. Maybe he showed them that
all men were not unfaithful. Maybe they would meet someone like him one day.

There was one more reason why he was looked on with
love and respect. Some boy friends who visited the hospital
frequently never greeted anyone else. They just talked and,
as I said, went to bed together in broad daylight. By contrast
Tadashi Maekawa would greet everyone on arrival, 'How
are you all? It's cold today, isn't it?' and, on leaving, 'Take
care of yourselves. Let me know if there is anything I can
get you in the town.' He would jot down requests for salted
herrings and salmon roe and such like, and never forgot the
things requested.

One day he phoned me. When I picked up the receiver in
the nurse's office he announced, 'I'm just going into town.
Would you ask the other patients if they want me to bring
them anything?'

The patients were probably all the more impressed because
it was snowing that day and commented, 'Isn't he kind? We
could learn something from him . . .'

There was a dark corridor in the hospital where couples
liked to meet, but Tadashi Maekawa would sit by my bed
discussing literature and the Bible, and then simply go home,
and they seemed to find this refreshing too. So the manner of
his visits struck them in one way or another, and when it

came to inviting his pastor no one hesitated or opposed it.

The day finally came. As I had a temperature my fellow-patients tried to relieve me of responsibility. One brought a table from the nurses' office and put a lace cloth on it. Another went to each room inviting people. Yet another bought and arranged flowers. Everyone worked hard.

There were six large rooms in our ward and nearly sixty patients. In one men's room they all said they were coming and were all delighted.

The children visited me from the paediatric department, where they ranged from pre-school to middle school in the large ward, and said seriously, 'When the pastor comes we would like him to come and talk to us too.' Involuntarily my heart warmed to them. The children who were not very ill in that department did nothing but run around the corridors shouting, yet those children had asked to hear the pastor speak. I was touched by this, and though I myself was still not a believer I longed that somehow one person would understand the Christian message and believe.

One lady of around fifty in my room exclaimed, 'Fancy me of all people meeting the pastor. I hope I won't be blinded!' and so saying she changed the sheets, put on her best kimono instead of her nightwear and was sitting upright on her bed with a tense face an hour before the pastor came. The other patients who knew little about Christianity all tidied up the place and, like the first lady, sat upright on their beds awaiting him.

The pastor is not God. He is an ordinary person. And though it was amusing to see them reverently greeting him as though he were God, I think it showed that there was a reverence for God in everyone's heart, and I could not laugh at that.

When he arrived, about thirty patients from other rooms had come to hear him speak. I think it was the evening of December 28th. But unfortunately what he said was too difficult for people hearing it for the first time, and consequently not very interesting. When he had gone the patients in my room discussed it.

'Christianity is terribly difficult, isn't it?'

'That's because everything is difficult at the beginning.'

'No, you can't understand that religion unless you're a scholar.'

Hearing this, the lady of about fifty who had said she wouldn't like to be blinded, said gravely, 'Whatever you say, now I have gazed upon the pastor's godly face, I feel refreshed and purified.'

As a result, although the subject was difficult they decided they would like to meet once a week to hear a talk. No one had a Bible. They bought them from the church and most people scrambled to get one. In one male ward all ten men bought Bibles.

So from the New Year onwards they had a regular visit from the pastor. One young man who played the guitar well began to practise hymns, and after the evening meal we began practising singing the hymns in my room, so that everyone could sing at the next meeting.

This regular meeting was an excellent stimulus for patients who had been idling away the time. When the men came around to chat they began to discuss life.

One evening the pastor was unable to come. Those who had assembled read the Bible and sang hymns and then I took the lead in a discussion on why people came to the meeting.

They all became serious as they put forward various ideas. Among them one older man remarked, 'I came to kill time.' It was so honest I bore it in mind.

There was a young man sitting with him. When he went along the corridor he always wore a coat over his nightclothes and he had a refined look, somewhat like Tadashi Maekawa. He seemed to write *haiku*,[21] for sometimes he came to our room about them. He said he came for cultural reasons, to broaden his mind. His name was Tsutomu Kuroe.

'But faith and culture are different,' I thought. At first

---

[21] Poems of 17 syllables.

everyone thought faith and culture and morals were the same.

One patient in that ward actually thought the Bible should be re-written.

'You should remove all the miracle stories from the Bible. If you just collect the verses such as "Love your enemies" and "Do not look on a woman with lust", I think modern people will read it.'

Everyone said they enjoyed the meeting that night and it was continued even when I moved to another hospital shortly afterwards.

Two months after the meetings started I was really taken by surprise. The man who said he was 'killing time' had read through the New Testament twice and wanted to be baptised. He and Tsutomu Kuroe worked for the Hokkaido Prefectural Police, though in different branches.

It was remarkable enough that he had read the New Testament twice in two months, but in addition he had learnt the names of many biblical characters. 'The Acts of the Apostles struck me more than the Gospels,' he commented. 'When I read of how Stephen was struck and killed and the Apostles suffered to spread the Gospel, I knew that Jesus Christ was God.' He had been deeply impressed.

I was amazed at his capacity for reading, and I was also amazed at the astonishing power of the Bible. Of all the patients at the discussion he alone had said he had come to kill time. It showed me that whatever motives people had when they read the Bible, they could be struck by its words. I was convinced that even if they read the Bible and did not understand it, or even if they were hostile towards it, it was extremely important to recommend the Bible to them. As for the results of this meeting, Tsutomu Kuroe and Rië believed and were baptised some years later. Tsutomu Kuroe became an earnest Christian, taking responsibility in the church, and continues to be active in evangelism even today.

26

I spent four months in that hospital, but my fever continued and I went on losing weight, though they could find no cause for it. I was sometimes up seven or eight times during the night. But when I reported this to the doctor, to my surprise he simply informed me that he would give me medicine to reduce the frequency.

I was an amateur in medical matters, but I expected him at least to give me a test. If he blindly prescribed medicine I could see my stay in hospital would be a lengthy business. How could I trust a doctor who simply treated the immediate symptoms? Surely above all else he ought to find the cause of my fever and prescribe the appropriate treatment. But this was not my only reason for leaving the hospital.

Recently my back had become curiously painful when I moved. I got the hospital surgeon to examine me, but he announced, 'It's nerves. A lot of young women have backache. You needn't take any notice of it.'

As it was so painful I asked if it could be spinal tuberculosis. The doctor was even more angry.

'There is nothing unusual on the X-ray. It's nerves.'

I had no alternative but to return to the ward.

I had been ill for seven years and ought to have been credited with ability to look at my condition objectively by then. No matter what the doctor said, I guessed from the symptoms that it was tuberculosis of the spine. Other patients with this disease had told me that the doctors made a wrong diagnosis any number of times, and usually when it was finally diagnosed they asked, 'Why didn't you come to hospital earlier?' According to them, when the patient's symptoms were genuine the X-ray would bear it out, but in spite of symptoms, if there was no shadow on the X-ray the doctor would not diagnose a tubercular spine. At all events the X-ray seemed to me more like superstition. To ignore the patient's symptoms and make the X-ray the deciding factor struck me as futile.

At last I decided to move to another hospital in Sapporo, because a close friend of Tadashi Maekawa's worked there. It needed courage to decide to move. Firstly, as my family were not prosperous it was a considerable burden, for my younger brother was still at high school. However, fortunately the health insurance system had changed at the bank where my father worked and the whole family were provided for. This came just at the right time and made me somewhat easier in my mind. I say somewhat, because I was not entirely happy. It was not a matter of simply meeting the hospital fees. The unseen miscellaneous expenses were considerable. Miserably I wondered if it were right to go on living like this, causing my parents so much trouble, and it was Tadashi Maekawa who spurred me on by scolding me!

'Aya-chan! It's not a question of having no right to live, we have an obligation to live. Your duty is just like the Chinese character says, in the ideograph for "obligation". It means doing the right thing.'

This remark encouraged me. Was it true? Was it my duty to live? If it were, then I must live no matter how much I suffered. I had felt presumptuous, living as a financial burden up to this point, but if this could be called my duty then it could even become a matter of quiet, humble acceptance.

But I also hesitated to change hospitals because it meant I must leave Asahikawa and Tadashi Maekawa. How much his daily visits had encouraged me while I was in hospital! To go to Sapporo where I knew no one, was bound to be lonely. I was uneasy, not knowing whether it would help my illness or when I would be able to return home.

At this point Tadashi Maekawa looked at me and smiled.

'Aya-chan,' he said, 'the time has come for you to live without relying on me or anybody else, because as long as you are living in dependence on others you cannot really live. You've got to make up your mind to depend on God.'

But while he said this he also admitted it was wretched to

know no one, and he sent a postcard to a Mr Nishimura, an elder of a Sapporo church. I knew nothing about him.

Miss Ayako Hotta, a seeker from Asahikawa church, is going into hospital in your city. Please do what you can for her.

Looking at the card that he had written for me, I wondered if on the basis of such a postcard this man would really visit an unknown sick person he had never set eyes on before, and I did not stake too much on it.

The evening before I moved, my younger brother Akio came to help me pack. He was a kindly brother and later visited me very often. My older sister Yuriko and Tadashi Maekawa came to say goodbye, and the other patients in my room made my favourite chicken soup on the charcoal burner we used. Rië-chan felt so lonely she ate nothing all day. The only lining I had for my collar was torn and another friend patched it with a new towel. I was moved to find they regretted my leaving although I had only been with them four months. The men patients brought me old newspapers for packing and ran errands to get things from the shop. Everyone was kind. I longed for the Christian meeting to continue after I left. As the leader I wanted to pass on the baton to someone else, and I entrusted this important task to Tsutomu Kuroe. He undertook it willingly, promising he would do the best he could.

The day before I left, another lady, the only one in our room with spinal tuberculosis, cried all day. She was a widow with two children and received social and medical assistance. Suddenly she was notified that social assistance would be cut off. There was no way to comfort her, unless this assistance continued.

I remembered from my teaching days a certain lecturer who had struck me as a generous person. Without thinking I immediately telephoned his house, and when I explained the lady's circumstances, he readily co-operated, and came round to the hospital immediately. Through his efforts this widow was helped, and many years after that he was also a great help to me.

At all events, without my being aware of it, a great change had taken place in me. At one time I had thought only of myself and now I could be seriously concerned for other people.

Early the next morning Tadashi Maekawa came to the station to see me off. He gave me a notebook.

'When you're lonely write something in here. We may be separated but we won't drift apart.'

It was February in Asahikawa and extremely bleak. That morning there were 20°C of frost.

And so I finally moved away from Tadashi Maekawa to live in another city. Wondering whether the move to Sapporo would cure my illness I blew on the frozen train window to melt the ice. Through the small hole in the frost I saw Tadashi Maekawa bow slightly as the train pulled out.

The New Way

27

THE DOCTOR WHO had been Tadashi Maekawa's contemporary was assistant professor at a medical college hospital in Sapporo. He was pale, with a rather detached air for a doctor, but I did not dislike his neat, cool manner. Indeed, it had a certain charm.

He did not give me the usual tests and X-ray as soon as I arrived, but let me rest. However, the following day he said there would be a fluid excretion test. It was a good thing for me that they had to conduct the test from the first day, because it left me no time to dwell on my loneliness away from Tadashi Maekawa and Asahikawa.

But even so, that first night I gazed out of the window at the Sapporo sky. It goes without saying that the weather in Sapporo was mild, for even with central-heating it would have been unthinkable to open a window and look out in the Asahikawa winter. The sky over the distant town was clear, and when I remembered there was no one I knew in this vast city my spirits somehow rose.

I was certainly lonely without Tadashi Maekawa but I found it a tremendous relief to know no one. Gazing across Sapporo by night, I wondered how many people I would get to know. I had let down all the people I had associated with in Asahikawa during my twenty or more years there. I longed with all my heart to make a fresh start in Sapporo and be faithful to my friends.

By chance I suddenly remembered Yasuhiko Mafuji.

After all, he should be there. I had never written to him but we had not completely severed our friendship. I firmly believed that in this existence man cannot sever his connections with his past self quite so simply. Even if I thought I had cut myself off from it all, I could never erase my previous actions. And if I died, the effects of those actions and my haphazard life would remain.

The illusion of relief which had come over me was strange and short-lived. The memory of my disloyalty to so many friends in the past began coiling itself around me and I turned away from the window.

Then, sitting on my bed, I opened my Bible. There were three of us in the room and my bed was nearest the corridor. The other two were already sleeping quietly. When I opened the Bible the following words caught my eye. 'Heaven and earth will pass away, but my words will not pass away.'[1]

Was this a pure coincidence? I was astonished at how relevant these words were to what I had just been thinking. They were saying that even though everything in the earth passed away and was destroyed, Jesus Christ's words would never in all eternity suffer the same fate. What did it mean? My finger stopped motionless on the page and I sat thinking. If Jesus' words would never be destroyed, then surely my own ugliness would also remain as long as the world lasted. If Jesus could say He forgave, then my sins could be forgiven, but if He did not forgive, then my sins would never be erased, for all eternity.

'Heaven and earth shall pass away, but my words shall not pass away.' Quietly I repeated these words and that night, along with the news about the new hospital, I added a postscript to Tadashi Maekawa about this.

Letters came from him as always. They were long letters, more detailed than when I was in Asahikawa. He gave me all the details of his life, the time he got up, the books he read, the people he met, and what they talked about. When I read all about his discussion with a friend on peace problems, or the acquisition of newly-published books at the

[1] Luke 21: 33.

T–D

bookshop, they were so graphically described that I ached with loneliness at being away from Asahikawa. He also said he was planning a visit to Sapporo for a check-up in March. Simply knowing he would come in March made every day happy for me. My happiness was filled with expectation and hope.

At this point a small incident took place. There was a phone call from Asahikawa and I went to the nurses' office. I picked up the receiver uneasily, wondering if something were wrong at home or if Tadashi Maekawa had made a mistake, but the call was from one of the men patients at the Asahikawa hospital who used to come and talk each evening. He was very agitated.

'Hello, is Rië-chan there?'

'Rië-chan? Is anything wrong?'

'Well, she received permission to go out of the hospital and said she was going home, but when a phone call came from her home we realised she hadn't gone there. Her mother and elder sister have left for Sapporo in case she visits you. If she arrives, please don't let her leave.'

Soon afterwards Rië-chan arrived in the ward with sparkling eyes and a thoughtful face. Sternly I asked, 'What have you come for?'

When I decided to change hospitals Rië-chan had become listless and would not eat. Such pining was touching, but I never revealed this to her. She had tried to commit suicide once and the scar had not yet fully healed. She had promised not to try a second time but, when you think of it, it was wretched for her to be parted from the one person in whom she had at last been able to confide.

Once she had been to Sapporo and seen me, she was happy and returned alone before her mother arrived. I was worried lest the hospital forcibly discharge her for deceiving them, so I telephoned and asked them not to make an issue of it, as she had not yet fully recovered emotionally from the suicide attempt. The hospital seemed to be fully aware of this and she continued there without a reprimand.

Through this incident I realised afresh the responsibility

of having friends. To love other people was to help them to stand on their own feet. This was what Tadashi Maekawa had said about me, when he urged, 'You've got to make up your mind to depend on God.'

The real love of parent for child and man for woman may be the love that makes the other person independent spiritually. When we say 'I cannot live without you' we probably do not yet know the discipline of real love. Be that as it may, through this matter of Rië, I felt I had learned the discipline of love and the responsibility of friendship.

28

With all this happening, the first week in hospital passed rapidly. One day a very neat, intelligent-looking nurse came to my room and explained in a clear voice, 'I'm Kazue Ochi from the E.N.T. Department. Nishimura-sensei telephoned to say that he had had a card from Tadashi Maekawa in Asahikawa asking him to visit you. He plans to come on Friday and hopes you are getting on all right in the meanwhile.'

To tell the truth, I was a little surprised. Tadashi Maekawa went to a church in Asahikawa and did not know Nishimura-sensei of Sapporo well. As four or five hundred members attended the morning service at Nishimura-sensei's church in Sapporo, they could not even know each other by sight. As one of the leaders of such a large church, Nishimura-sensei would be extremely busy, just with church matters. In addition he was head of a bakery which employed several hundred people, he had opened a cake shop opposite the station and was running a teashop and restaurant. I could imagine how busy he was with that alone and wondered why, at the request of Tadashi Maekawa whom he scarcely knew, he was coming to see someone he had never before seen or heard of. Usually we can scarcely find time to visit our own friends and acquaintances.

But, contrary to my expectations, Nishimura-sensei appeared in my room the following Friday. He was a large friendly man of fifty-five or so. He had big eyes but they were set in a cheerful face.

'I wanted to visit you as soon as I received the card from Tadashi Maekawa in Asahikawa and I'm sorry for the delay,' he explained, and looking around the room he held out a box of cakes.

'So, there are three of you in the room. Please share these cakes with the others. The *choux* cream doesn't keep, so eat them first.'

Without taking the cakes I answered, 'I've been sick a long time. When people visit me I never expect them to bring gifts. When people get used to receiving things from others they become greedy. Please don't bring me gifts.'

I was stubborn, and had warned myself that if I got used to receiving things from people I would turn into a scrounger. Besides, Nishimura-sensei was a total stranger at this point and under no obligation at all to visit me. I could not bring myself to receive gifts from him. He looked surprised. Later I discovered that, busy as he was, he set apart Friday and Sunday for Christian service. What with explaining the Bible to employees of the Hokkaido Government office and the hospital, and visiting the sick, Friday and Sunday were tightly packed. I don't know how many he must have visited up to that point, but I doubt if anyone had turned on him when they first met as I did, saying, 'Please don't bring me gifts.'

He laughed out loud. 'Yes, yes, I understand. But Hotta-san, when you enjoy the sunshine every day, do you ration yourself by saying, "Shall I enjoy it from this angle or that?"'

I was silent. If the sun shone I did not thank or reject it, but basked in it without a thought. Weren't people's gifts like the sunshine, the outpouring of their love for me? I ought to accept it with good grace and gratitude. Actually, having been sick for many years I had been blessed by the love of so many people, starting with my parents, brothers and sisters. This was probably why I announced so patronisingly that I did not need gifts. I was ashamed.

Nishimura-sensei was not a pastor, but everyone addressed him as such and he was certainly a remarkable person. However impertinent I was, he was generous enough to take it all in his stride. I would like to tell you more about him.

Actually he had wanted to become a pastor, but his own pastor thought he should abandon the idea. His family's financial circumstances were such that if he as the eldest son became a pastor it would cause them too much hardship. A Japanese pastor works hard for little material reward. Even now there are some pastors who lead a hand-to-mouth existence. In 1936 pastors lived in even greater poverty.

Nishimura-sensei's desire to become a pastor permeated his whole life, however, and he became an exceptional Christian. When he was a teacher at the Commercial School, he visited a student who was critically ill and on leaving the room he wept in the corridor, 'I've been teaching him English every day and I never taught him anything about the most important things in life. Now I cannot bring him what he needs most.'

The student died, but from that time Nishimura began to spend an hour every morning before work explaining the Bible to interested students. As a result of those talks many of them became Christians and were baptised. They say that thanks to him, the whole spirit of the Commercial School was changed.

Because of family circumstances he gave up teaching and opened a cake shop. I heard that one third of the profits he used for other people, one third for running expenses, and the remaining third for his own living expenses. I have written at length about him because he came to wield an enormous influence on me.

As I became accustomed to life in the new hospital I found myself being enveloped for a second time in nihilistic thinking. I often thought that no matter what I did, it was futile. My thoughts centred entirely on myself. Could people like me really become Christians? Was God so large-hearted He could forgive someone like me?

Then one day Ichiro Nishinaka, my former fiancé, visited me unexpectedly. He was married and living in Ebetsu. He commuted daily to a commercial company in Sapporo.

'It's been a long time. How did you know I was here?' I asked.

I spoke freely, as if to someone I met daily, but it was our first reunion since I had tried to take my life on that dark seashore. At that time I had had strength enough to withstand nearly ten hours of swaying in the train. Now I was so weak that merely walking down the ward left me breathless.

'Ichiro-san, you've got married, haven't you? Congratulations!'

After waiting several years for me he had married a healthy girl, and I was glad. He had the ability to make somebody happy and I wanted him to be happy.

He looked at me in silence, and then said solemnly, 'You're a good person.'

Maybe he was surprised that a woman who was still ill could wish her former fiancé well when he married.

'Ichiro-san, there is someone I want to introduce you to.' And so saying I glanced up at a poem of Tadashi Maekawa's hanging nearby. Ichiro Nishinaka would not let me say anything about him.

'Aya-chan, I don't want to hear anything. The Aya-chan I know is enough for me.'

My engagement to Ichiro Nishinaka was for me a thing of the past, but it seemed as if in his heart I was not entirely relegated to the past. I did not venture to say more about Tadashi Maekawa.

Ichiro Nishinaka looked at my face attentively.

'You've got thin, haven't you?'

'How old is your wife? I hope she is well.'

It wasn't painful to ask. If I had not caught tuberculosis I would probably have married him and by now we would have had a couple of children and I would have had the joy of motherhood. Thinking of this as I watched him, I thought how strange human relationships were and asked a second time, 'But how did you know I was here?'

He said he had caught sight of me as he passed the hospital. He had brought me some tinned food, fruit and paper tissues. 'I thought you would find them useful,' he said. When he had visited me before he was always kind and attentive, holding the sputum cup for me when I coughed. So he reappeared in my life for a second time, as kindly as ever.

29

I had moved to this hospital but here too they could discover nothing wrong with either my chest or spine. They examined me thoroughly and as at Asahikawa could find no reason for my loss of weight or temperature. But whereas the other hospital had treated its patients rather casually, this one at least took things seriously and the patients could trust them and relax.

One day in March, a month after I moved, I was staring listlessly at the sky around noon. My bed was by the window by then. I was thinking how mild and spring-like the sky was, when suddenly the bed began to shake. With a start I sat up.

The other two patients woke with the cry, 'Earthquake!'

The building began to rock in an uncanny way and in a flash a crack appeared in the white wall in front of us. The agitated voices of nurses and patients sounded from the corridor.

The earthquake soon passed, but it had been a frightening experience. Asahikawa, where I had been born and bred, had very few earthquakes and we were seldom aware of even a tremor, so the solid earth was about the only thing that did not frighten me. This protracted earthquake literally terrified me. My heart cried out, 'There is nowhere on earth completely safe!' For the first time I became aware of how I had taken safety for granted, in a world which was quite uncertain.

When I thought this over, I came to realise that just as we enjoy a sense of security on fickle *terra firma*, so we also find it in ephemeral things. For some people it is in money, for others health and for others status, but these are even more unreliable than the solid earth. Our physical existence can never be wholly secure.

So then I wondered what basis for a sense of security I really had. I could see no reason why I should find it in anything. Rather I ought to feel apprehensive, unable to trust in anything. But I had to admit that fundamentally this had never before worried me. Now if I really had nothing to rely on, I should become a more determined seeker, looking for true peace of mind. I began to see the contradictions of my position. I was half-hearted in my searching because I had been feeling secure even when I was in danger.

The Bible, which I had read at random so far, I now began to read seriously. I constantly prepared questions in readiness for Nishimura-sensei's periodical visits and listened eagerly to what he said, unwilling to waste any part of such a busy person's time.

It was a pity for me to monopolise him. I was told he was such an eloquent speaker that if he preached in the street several hundred people would stop and none went away. What he said always made a deep impression, and no-one knows how many people he led to Christ.

Even though I was the only patient he visited in that hospital, he taught me most painstakingly. In his cordial way he answered my many questions, constantly quoting from the Bible, and as a result I was able to get a clear grasp of its most important teaching. This was a great help to me. He also asked, 'Do you have any relative or friend who can help you while you are in Sapporo?'

When I answered that I had no one he said again,

'Well then, please let us help you. Please tell us of anything you want.'

Accordingly he took the place of a relative to me and I cannot number his kindnesses as he washed out the dirty, blood-stained sputum mug, or travelled from his house nearly a mile away to bring me hot food. Time and again I was impressed with what a remarkable person he was for the head of a company with several hundred employees.

Through his character and all he said I gradually came to understand Christianity more fully, and even began to think about being baptised.

But men's hearts are not all alike. Tadashi Maekawa with his love, Nishimura-sensei with his genuineness, both were remarkable even amongst Christians. Loved and guided by such people, it would have been no wonder if I had soon become a Christian. But things did not go smoothly for me and Ichiro Nishinaka was one reason for this.

30

About that time Ichiro Nishinaka began to visit me daily and as he came at the same time each day unconsciously I came to look forward to his regular appearance. He worked very near to the hospital so he dropped in at noon. He and Nishimura-sensei were the only visitors I had. I could not help finding his visits enjoyable for he was the only daily visitor, and even if he had been a woman I would have looked forward to them.

The money I received from home was just enough to meet my hospital expenses without leaving me so much as to buy an orange. Tadashi Maekawa, looking for a way to earn money to pay for the postcards he sent me, learned to print stencils by hand but, of course, in such circumstances I could not look to him to send me money. He often wrote,

For your sake I want to return to hospital and qualify as a doctor as soon as possible. It is so wretched for a man to see someone he loves in financial straits.

The day the professor came round, the ward orderly did the cleaning with special care and urged the patients to change their night-clothes. Any number of times she must have said to me, 'Hotta-san, the doctor comes today. Please change your clothes.' However often she said it, I only had one night kimono. As I had never taken much interest in clothes that was no great hardship, but even to this day I cannot forget how I had to change into an under-garment while someone washed my kimono for me.

In these circumstances Ichiro Nishinaka's visits helped me in various ways. When I had no paper tissue, over and over again he brought me surplus paper from his firm's store. For my heavy coughing this strong paper was better than tissue. Moreover, remembering my likes and dislikes from so many years before, he would arrive with an orange slipped into his pocket and tins of food. Yet, in spite of his daily visits there was no suggestion of anything deeper between us. Ichiro Nishinaka was a person with high standards of integrity.

He had certainly not wanted to hear about Tadashi Maekawa on his first visit, but not because he expected anything of me himself. His inherent kindness would not let him lose sight of his former fiancée, sick and needy in a strange place, as the following incident shows. I had become unable to bend because of the pain in my back from the previous year. When I wanted to pick up something that had dropped on the floor, I had to do so by kneeling down gently, keeping my back straight. Because of this I was quite unable to wash my feet let alone have a bath. The hospital was probably short-handed, because the nursing orderly was always too busy serving meals and cleaning to help me wash myself. I think it was part of her responsi-bility but there were so many surgical cases in the depart-ment that she had no time to help those who could walk around.

Unable to bear the sight of me in this condition, one day Ichiro Nishinaka brought a bucket of hot water from the boiler room and said he was going to wash my feet. I refused to accept his kindness, saying, 'Ichiro-san, are you as great as Jesus ? Well then, you're not worthy to wash people's feet.'

There is an account in the Bible of how Jesus washed the feet of his twelve disciples the night before he died on the cross.

Although I had rejected his kindness he chatted as usual, quite as if nothing had happened, and went home. If he had had any secret designs, why would he have wanted to wash my feet ? And in front of the other patients, too. This episode revealed his genuine kindness, free of any trace of intrigue, and I remember being deeply impressed.

For this reason I never heard any embarrassing gossip about the two of us, but eventually I came up against a serious truth. One night the lady in the next bed confided to me with a dejected face,

'It seems as if my husband has taken a girl at work out for coffee. When I mentioned it to him he answered, "What's wrong with that?" and shrugged it off. But I think it's horrid. Don't you?'

'Yes, I do. Even if he says there is nothing in it, for him to hobnob with another woman in a café isn't nice. It makes me angry to think about it, and when you're in hospital too . . .', I answered sympathetically. What would I feel if Tadashi Maekawa took another young girl out for coffee while I was in hospital in Sapporo? Even if it were only an isolated incident I would find it quite unbearable.

Then, as I thought about it, I was dumbfounded. What right had I to say that it would be unpleasant if Tadashi Maekawa went to a café with another girl? Wasn't I receiving daily visits from Ichiro Nishinaka? However innocent it was, we had been engaged to be married and now he had a wife and I had Tadashi Maekawa.

I had told Tadashi Maekawa about Ichiro Nishinaka's visits and, though he had not mentioned the matter at all, I could not be sure that it was not unpleasant for him. And if Ichiro Nishinaka's wife knew about it she might well be hurt. I had never been conscious of hurting anyone like that before, but as the lady in the next bed whispered, 'I don't like it, I don't like it,' and I watched her lying sleepless that night, she seemed to be Ichiro Nishinaka's wife.

For the first time I became aware of how wrong my behaviour had been. If I had become aware of it, then I ought to stop Ichiro Nishinaka's visits immediately. But when he arrived to see me the next day I decided there was nothing particularly wrong about it. He loved his wife and I loved Tadashi Maekawa. Defiantly I asked myself what was wrong in being friends in this way? If his wife or Tadashi Maekawa were troubled about it I felt I could even reply with a laugh, 'Don't be silly! Worry about something more serious!'

Looking back at it objectively, I might well have been wounding one of them, but at the time it never occurred to me that I was doing anything so wrong. Far from that, I only wanted this warm friendship with Ichiro Nishinaka to continue as it was. I suppose I just did not want to lose the kindly friendship of such a person as he.

And then I suddenly became afraid of myself. Supposing the trouble was that I lacked all consciousness of sin? Was it a terrible thing for me not to be conscious of sin? A murderer would not care, a thief would have no pangs of conscience, and in the same way I also felt no grief for wounding another person by my actions. I began wondering whether it was not the greatest sin of all to be unaware of one's sin. And then I felt I had begun to understand the significance of the crucifixion of Jesus Christ.

31

Spring in Sapporo seemed to come two weeks ahead of Asahikawa. It was April, Sapporo's characteristic spring dust storms were blowing, and I was growing steadily thinner.

When I went to see an elderly physician in out-patients, he applied the stethoscope and said, 'There it is. There's the cavity.' Facing me again he remarked, 'I can hear it quite

clearly through the stethoscope, so there's no reason to
suppose that it won't be visible on an X-ray.'

This hospital and the previous one and the sanatorium
had all said that there was no cavity on the X-ray; but I
had this temperature, my shoulders ached, my sputum was
bloodstained and of such quantity that I never had enough
paper tissues. The doctor made immediate arrangements for
an X-ray and as a result he found the cavity, six centimetres
inside. A lady doctor has remarked that his stethoscope
must have been the ear of God himself. I was moved to the
medical ward and the doctor said he would operate when I
had gained weight.

On the other hand the pain in my back grew steadily
worse. It became difficult to slip my feet into my slippers.
After two or three steps I began to stagger. My slight
knowledge of the symptoms of spinal tuberculosis were
enough to make me very apprehensive. Surely these were
the symptoms of that disease. If nothing was done I faced
the awful consequences of being paralysed from the waist
down and becoming incontinent.

Soon I had another X-ray taken, but the young doctor
announced, 'It's all right. There's nothing on the X-ray.'
I was angry. They had said no cavity was to be seen on the
chest X-ray when my symptoms were well advanced, until
eventually one doctor had discovered the cavity with his
stethoscope. Why were doctors so stubbornly turning a
deaf ear to the patient's complaints and repeating the same mis-
takes time and again? And as if that were not enough, they
cynically labelled such complaints as neurotic. I no longer
had any faith in X-rays. Since the patient's symptoms were
present long before anything appeared on the screen, surely
the X-ray was not simply useless but downright dangerous.

I had a second spinal X-ray at the end of May. This time
the doctor protested, 'Why didn't you get us to investigate
this before? You have spinal tuberculosis. You need absolute rest in a plaster cast.'

The doctor at out-patients changed from day to day. I
burst out laughing at what this one said.

'What's the matter?'

I had heard that some patients cried when spinal tuberculosis was diagnosed, yet I had laughed. No wonder the doctor was puzzled. But I was laughing because now I could relax, instead of being treated as neurotic and told, 'It's all imaginary. Why don't you get up and get some exercise?'

Once they knew the root cause, there was a way to treat it.

Back in my room I thought hard. Although my spine was being eaten away by tuberculosis and I stumbled as I walked, we had been blind to its presence simply because it had not appeared on the X-ray. If this ignorance had continued, might not all my bones have been affected? I would certainly have died.

And then I thought, 'The same could be true of my soul.' Maybe I did not realise my heart was being eaten away or how infected I was, simply because I was unaware of my sin. I found this thought very frightening.

My mind was made up. I had come to an end of myself. I wanted to clinch my decision by being baptised as soon as possible.

Nishimura-sensei was overjoyed to hear of it. 'It's just as you say. We don't realise how fearful sin is. If we found we had leprosy we would rush to the doctor in alarm, but although we admit our sins we're in no hurry to go to God. I'm glad you want to be baptised.'

My baptism was arranged for July 5th. I was moved from the medical ward to the room for advanced cases because I was infectious. The medical ward had been pleasant but the new room was drab. The dirty worm-eaten pillars and the mildewed walls made the whole room dark. A farmer's wife of about fifty, her illness much more advanced than mine, was lying there gaunt in the same room.

Noticing that my bed smelt strongly of carbolic I asked the orderly, 'Has someone just died in this bed?'

It was as I thought. A woman in her sixties had died only a few hours before I was moved.

'That's horrible, following a dead person.'

The dark-complexioned orderly sympathised gently, but I turned my face away. Was there one single person alive who would not die? Probably in this particular ward there was not a bed in which someone had not died. The person I had been up till now was going to die here too. As the Bible said, the 'old' me, so sinful through and through, must 'go' and I must begin my life all over again in Jesus Christ. 'When anyone is joined to Christ, he is a new being; the old is gone, the new has come.'[2]

It seemed appropriate that from now on I would spend my convalescence on the bed of a dead person.

32

At last July 5th, the day of my baptism, arrived. I had said nothing to my parents about it. Where religion was concerned they did not interfere, not so much from conviction as indifference. I had only told Tadashi Maekawa in Asahikawa.

It was a beautiful day. After lunch an attractive nurse came into the ward.

'I hear you're being baptised. Congratulations! I'll tidy up your room, shall I?'

She was a member of the same church as Nishimura-sensei in Sapporo. Quickly she tidied up and brought a chair from the office for the pastor, then Nurse Ochi came, a member of the same church.

At one o'clock, as arranged, Nishimura-sensei arrived with the pastor from another church. I had heard this pastor was a man of some spirit. He had been imprisoned during the war for advocating peace. I had also heard that he was extremely strict, but when I met him that day he was very gentle and quiet. I was proud to be baptised by a man of his calibre.

At last the baptismal service began. Nishimura-sensei held a special bowl of water; the only others present were the

[2] 2 Corinthians 5: 17.

two Christian nurses, and I lay as I was in the plaster cast. The pastor read from the sixth chapter of Romans, in the Bible,

'For surely you know this: when we were baptised into union with Christ Jesus, we were baptised into union with his death. By our baptism then we were buried with him and shared his death in order that just as Christ was raised from death by the glorious power of the Father, so also we might have new life.

'For if we became one with him in dying as he did, in the same way we shall become one with him by being raised alive as he was. For we know this: our old being has been put to death with Christ on his cross, in order that the power of the sinful self might be destroyed, so that we should no longer be slaves of sin. For when a person dies, he is set free from the power of sin. If we have died with Christ we believe we shall also live with him.'

Then the pastor dipped his hand in the water and placed it on my head.

'Ayako Hotta, I baptise you in the name of the Father, and of the Son, and of the Holy Spirit. Amen.'

Up to that point I had felt quite calm, even though I was taking the big step of being baptised. I was so calm I wondered uneasily if it were all right not to feel excited or deeply stirred. But as soon as I heard these words I suddenly found myself in tears. I was quite unprepared for this. I could not help weeping at the thought that someone as untrustworthy and sinful as I, could belong to Christ.

The pastor prayed: 'Heavenly Father, we thank you because you have allowed the name of this sick sister to be included in your Kingdom. Please bring her faith to perfection at the final day.'

Between my sobs I joined in the 'Amen'. Nishimura-sensei followed with a prayer. His eyes were moist too and his prayer was halting, but it was also a prayer of thanksgiving,

'Please use our sister Hotta-san to be a witness for you in

her present circumstances and, if it is your will, release her from her illness as soon as possible and use her in your work.'

Then we sang a hymn. The gist of it was, 'Lord Jesus, we sinners wandering on a dark journey rejoice to receive the light of your grace, which shines everywhere.'

Suddenly I recalled that night on the dark seashore when I was rescued by Ichiro Nishinaka. The words 'wandering on a dark journey' had certainly been true that night when I had no desire to live.

They sang on, 'Now this sinful self has died and risen through your power. I have been numbered with God's servants and baptism is the sign of my cleansing.'

The nurses' eyes were moist and I was so deeply moved that although fifteen years have passed since that time, my eyes fill whenever that hymn is sung.

When the service was over the pastor had to leave immediately for his next meeting. Quietly he said, 'You are definitely going to get better. This is just a time of testing.'

I nodded meekly. I did not look as if I would recover, but neither did I think his words were mere politeness. Men's words are precious. The tongue can kill or give life.

'You are definitely going to get better.' During the long years of sickness that followed, those quiet words, spoken with conviction, comforted and encouraged me many times. That was the only time I met that pastor, but the words I heard that once had power to comfort countless times later. And something strange happened. From the day I was baptised I was flooded with happiness. There was a hope burning in my heart and it stirred me.

Immediately I prayed, 'Oh, God, please let Yasuhiko-san and Rië-san become Christians. If these two become Christians I don't mind when you call me to heaven.'

Then I wrote cards to both of them. I could not help wanting to share the joy I experienced, just like having something specially tasty and wanting others to enjoy it too. It was hard writing postcards lying flat in a plaster cast, and my shoulders soon ached. It took a day or so to write one

card, but nothing could stop me from writing. When I considered Nishimura-sensei's routine, I could not forget that
a Christian must share the Good News. So, however painful
it was, I intended to go on writing to my friends.

A letter arrived from Tadashi Maekawa. Hearing of my
baptism, he said he had read Romans 6 by himself and sung
the same hymn and prayed with a heart full of thanksgiving.
It was Tadashi Maekawa who had struck his foot with a
stone for me on Shunkodai Hill. It was he whose daily
letters had led me to Christ. It was he who had made a
long detour home from church to stand under my window
secretly praying for me. The news of my baptism must have
brought him a joy no words could describe. Reading again
his description of how he had prayed alone for me, the tears
ran down my cheeks unchecked.

33

November came, and suddenly Tadashi Maekawa arrived
in Sapporo carrying a large suitcase. He put it down on the
floor, coughing, and said, 'Aya-chan, will you let me stay
here for a week?'[3]

'What's happened? Have you come for a check-up?'

A week's stay seemed too long for a check-up. He ignored
the question and remarked sympathetically,

'It must be awful for you. That plaster cast must be so
trying.'

I had not found the cast trying. Entirely encased in plaster
from head to hips, I could not even move my neck because if
I did it caused pain down my spine. It was certainly hard
being unable to move my head or turn over, but it was far
better than being told, 'You're not ill. Get some exercise!'
and being made to walk when I had a temperature and my
back ached.

When I answered, 'No, it isn't trying,' he remarked with a

[3] A relative or friend would often stay with a patient to help care for
them.

smile, 'You're coming on, now that you're a believer!'

'Yes. But tell me, why are you spending a week in Sapporo?'

It was wonderful to have him near, and staying in my room into the bargain. I had never envisaged such happiness, but for some reason I could not help feeling uneasy. We began to talk quietly so as not to disturb the farmer's wife who was so ill in the same room.

'Well, Aya-chan, I have finally decided to have surgery.'

I looked at him, astonished.

'Tadashi-san, why is an operation necessary? Isn't it better to wait a little longer?'

Such surgery was not uncommon at that time, but even so a fair percentage of people died soon afterwards.

'You may be thinking because I weigh ten stone I'll get better without surgery but, Aya-chan, if my lungs are left in this diseased condition I'll never get better.'

I looked at him in silence. He was giving me his decision as a medical student.

'I don't know if the operation will be successful or not. It's a chancy business but I thought I'd try. I can't go on nursing bad lungs for ever. If it's a success I can return to my studies and graduate in six months or so. But, what's more important, you're confined to a plaster cast and may have to lie here for a year or two. For your sake I want to qualify as a doctor as soon as possible, so that I can support you financially.'

I could only grasp that he was so ill he had to have a dangerous operation. My heart sank. Then I remembered something he had once said: 'a man who can do nothing to help the person he loves is miserable.'

He had left his family without telling them of his resolution to undergo surgery, and when I thought of his touching reason I could only nod silently. From that day until a bed became vacant he stayed in my room.

Tadashi Maekawa seemed very happy. When he got up in the morning he brought me hot water and washed my face.

Until he came, no one had washed me. The orderly placed a bowl of water on my chest and, trying not to spill it I gazed up at the ceiling as I washed my hands, wrung out the cloth and wiped my face clean. Thoughtfully he enquired, 'Do you use lotion or cream? Where is it?'

'I don't have either.'

During the day he went to the Mitsukoshi department store and bought me some cream.

'I don't know anything about cosmetics so I've bought you the kind my mother uses.'

So saying, he put the cream on my face — nose, forehead, chin, bit by bit smoothing it in with his fingers and murmuring with a twinkle, 'Be beautiful! Be beautiful!'

Suddenly there was a lump in my throat, and I prayed that his operation would be a success.

He took care of me devotedly, even helping me with meals, writing my letters, and changing my hot water bottle. When breakfast was over he used to sit by my pillow and read the Bible to me. After that he would sit quietly on the straw mat by the bed and read a favourite book or write poems. He was so quiet I had to use my mirror to see what he was doing. Then he diligently worked on the poems he had written, and when he realised I was watching him in my mirror his face would light up with a smile. So life was simple for us but we were quite content.

The evenings in hospital were long. By five o'clock the evening meal was over, and the nursing orderlies went home. We talked about the Bible and discussed novels and happily passed the time until the light went out at nine p.m. As that time drew near, we read the Bible again, as we had done in the morning, and then he spread his mattress on the floor-boards and lay down.

When the lights were out he stretched out his hand from below and timidly touched my hair. As a Christian, this caress was his deepest expression of affection for me.

Three or four days later he received a letter from his father. He read it in silence and then handed it to me.

'Would you like to read this?'

I hesitated. 'It would be disrespectful to your father to read something addressed to you.'

'It's all right. My father and I are very much alike. If you read it you will understand me better.' I glanced through the letter as he asked me. It was a rebuke for deciding on surgery without discussing it with his parents. I have forgotten the details, but the letter was full of affection:

'I have been very outspoken, but please don't take offence. I have only written out of concern for you.'

I was not surprised. Tadashi's decision on his own to undergo surgery, when he was dependent on his parents, could only be seen as a slight to them. Even if he knew he could not get their consent, he deserved criticism. So I was amazed that his father, while rightly reproving him, thoroughly respected his son's wish. I thought they were wonderful people.

At last, on the ninth day, a bed became vacant and he was formally admitted to hospital. These few days were the only time we were ever together day and night in the same room.

34

The day for Tadashi Maekawa's operation was finally fixed. I think it was December 17th. His mother came from Asahikawa to nurse him. She dropped in to visit me and sat quietly stroking my wasted hands. At that moment he came in and, seeing what his own mother was doing, he broke into a smile. It delighted him but, quite apart from that, he seemed to be extremely happy that day.

They had to remove eight ribs. Fortunately he was in the same ward and his room was not far away, but I could not even visit him, let alone care for him. I had never felt so keenly the misery of my own illness as I did then. Although this might well be the most dangerous experience of his life I could do nothing but pray.

The evening before the operation he had a bath and came to my room.

'I didn't wash one foot. The old folk threaten that if you wash yourself all over you will go to the next world. We men are weak. We say we believe in God and are not superstitious, but still I left just one foot unwashed!' He went on, 'I don't mind about the operation; it's the anaesthetic I don't like. They say you get delirious coming around from the anaesthetic. I don't want to disgrace you by waking up calling "Aya-chan, Aya-chan!"'

At this the woman in the next bed remarked, 'Men are like children, aren't they? Anyway, his operation will be a success.'

As a farmer's wife she belonged to an old-style, feudalistic family and had never even read a newspaper. Tadashi Maekawa would listen to her, however, as if she were one of his own family. With appropriate remarks such as 'Oh', and 'That's terrible', he treated her as he would anyone else and never laughed at her. I was particularly impressed when she accidentally lost her ring. He crawled under the bed and into the corners searching for it and he finally went through the bin by her bed with his bare hands. She was much worse than I was and the bin was full of blood-stained tissues. I was filled with admiration as he removed them one by one, as though he were carefully searching for something precious of his own. The ring never turned up, but the woman thought highly of him long afterwards.

'Someone as good as Tadashi Maekawa won't die after an operation,' she said again.

The next day his younger brother and a friend hurriedly arrived from Asahikawa. They told me he had gone down to the theatre. I was praying hard. The picture of the scalpel being applied to his back drifted before my eyes. I could see everything from the white fatty tissue under the skin to the movement of the lungs beneath the ribs as he breathed. Together with Tadashi I had once watched an operation on a friend and written an account of it in the TB patients' magazine. I remembered it all now, and felt I could even hear the sound of the ribs being excised. The minutes ticked by as the operation went on.

35

I was helpless in my plaster case — I could do nothing except pray. By and by a young nurse came to tell me the operation was over.

'Is he all right?'

'Well, he's still under the anaesthetic. He's asleep and looking rather pale.'

She answered frankly, as if unaware that I wanted her to say he was well, even if it was a lie.

When I judged he should have come round from the anaesthetic I asked the orderly to go and see if he was awake and to enquire how he was. His room was so near, the whole thing only took a minute.

'It's strange. He hasn't woken up yet. He should be getting restless by now.'

Whereas I was merely uneasy before, now I was panic stricken. Only a few days earlier I had heard of someone who had died without recovering from the anaesthetic. However much I tried I could not control my fear.

Two hours later they told me that he had come round from the anaesthetic at last. As I folded my hands to offer a prayer of joy and thanksgiving there was no strength in my fingers. Later someone remarked, 'Maekawa-san is a real gentleman. When he came round from the anaesthetic he didn't get violent like most people do.'

All the same, there seemed to be something strange about the anaesthetic or its administration. Anaesthesia has made tremendous progress since that time.

I heard that he was recovering slowly. Then one night, some ten days after the operation, I saw the door open and for a moment I was startled as a wraith-like figure came in. Was it a ghost? The moment I realised it was Tadashi Maekawa, I was in tears before I could open my mouth. Had his suffering made him so thin?

During those painful days I had been imprisoned in bed,

unable to visit him. Although I had no option, it still seemed so heartless.

'Is it all right for you to be walking around?'

But he was not as serious as I was. With a lighthearted smile he replied, 'Well actually, this is the first time I've been to the toilet. My mother doesn't know I've called in here at the same time.'

Those who have never been ill will not realise that even so short a walk is quite exhausting when you are so weak. It was tiring enough for him to walk for the first time, even without coming to my room. He sat on a chair in silence as if it set his heart at rest just to see my face. He was probably too exhausted to talk. Before long a nurse found him and scolded him and he returned unsteadily to bed.

At last the year drew to a close. Tadashi Maekawa had undergone surgery and I had been baptised, so 1953 was unforgettable for both of us. And then the New Year came. His mother cooked ham and eggs to celebrate and brought me some. We were greeting the New Year together in the same hospital. I suddenly wondered whether he too was welcoming the New Year with ham and eggs.

No sooner had I breathed a sigh of relief than his second operation followed two weeks later. To remove the eight ribs they performed two operations, removing four at a time. It seemed so pitiful that he must go through the same suffering a second time, but deep in my heart I felt that if he had come safely through the first operation the second would be all right too. So I was not as anxious as I had been before, and yet I could not bear the thought that he must endure so much, just as he had regained a little of his strength.

I recalled the time when I had been ready to throw my own life away. Yet he had to go through all this suffering to regain his health. At long last I understood how wrong it had been to despise the gift of life, and I repented of my foolishness.

It was the morning after his second operation. As I lay dozing in bed I thought his mother and younger brother came in. They said they had come to return the mat they had borrowed. I had lent it to his mother to put on the floor. Astonished I exclaimed, 'But you still need it.'

'Tadashi has just died so we won't need it again,' and the the two of them gripped my bed, weeping.

I tried to cry out, 'He can't have done,' but no words came. When I felt I could speak at last, I opened my eyes. This was far too vivid to have been a dream and I had a sense of foreboding I could not describe. I felt I had seen an unpleasant vision, rather than an ordinary nightmare.

But contrary to my dream, the second time he regained his strength day by day and was able to leave hospital at the end of March. When his father came to fetch him and visited me, my eyes were red and swollen with crying. I should have been happier than anyone that he had safely undergone a serious operation and was returning home well but instead I could do nothing but cry and cry.

Was it because I was far from Asahikawa, alone and ill in Sapporo? Was it the sorrow of parting, after spending five months together in hospital? I did not even know myself, but my tears flowed and flowed. Or were these tears also an omen of unhappiness? At last he returned to Asahikawa.

> We read the Bible together and settle down to sleep.
> Tomorrow I go away, leaving you in bed.
>   Tadashi Maekawa

36

A month later, at the end of April, when Nishimura-sensei called, his usually cheerful face seemed strangely drawn. It was a somewhat misty day and rather cold. After reading the Bible and talking about it, he announced,

'I have to go to Tokyo next month.'

I knew he was a member of some committee down there. Only later I heard that, because he was already overworked, his lungs were congested and he had been ordered complete rest, but at the time I knew nothing of this and casually remarked,

'You'll be travelling first class then.'

'No! I hate the prim atmosphere of first class. In second class I can talk to anyone freely and then it's easier to talk about Jesus. If I had the money for first class I could put it to better use,' and he laughed.

As usual he straightened the quilt on my bed as he left. It kept sliding off.

A fortnight later I heard that Nishimura-sensei had been taken ill and had come back from Tokyo by sleeper. Anxiously I wondered how serious it was if he had returned by sleeper when he would not travel first class.

May passed into June, but Nishimura-sensei did not come to see me. I sent a letter and he wrote back telling me not to worry.

On July 5th, the first anniversary of my baptism came around. As I prayed I recalled the events of that day. The pastor who had baptised me was now ill with a cerebral haemorrhage. I thought of his words, 'You are definitely going to get better.' and I thought of Nishimura-sensei praying for me with tears. The pastor was seriously ill and Nishimura-sensei seemed to be making little progress. One never knew what would happen in the short space of a year.

Two or three days later there was a letter from Nishimura-sensei. He had noticed in the church bulletin that I had sent a thank-offering on the anniversary of my baptism. He knew how difficult it was to find the money when I was ill, and it must have given him much joy, after all his help and countless visits. It was a very happy letter. I intended to write back immediately but I was moved to another ward and was tired. On July 11th a student who was lodging at his house appeared and announced.

'Sensei is extremely ill.'

'I don't believe you,' I exclaimed indignantly. I thought he was teasing me.

He was a member of a church in Asahikawa and a friend of Tadashi Maekawa. That spring he had entered Hokudai

University and asked me if I knew where he could get lodgings and do some work. When I mentioned it to Nishimura-sensei's wife she had replied very cheerfully, 'He can stay with us if he wants to.' As I had acted as go-between for him it was quite possible that he was teasing me.

I was still fuming after he had gone, but when I enquired from Nurse Ochi she remarked, 'I didn't want to tell you, but the nurse is staying there day and night.'

Nurse Ochi was a very kind, cheerful person. Every Monday without fail she brought me the church bulletin and went over the pastor's sermon.

The following day, July 12th, was a Sunday. It was a beautiful day, hot enough to make me perspire even though I was lying still. As almost eighteen months had passed since I was admitted to the hospital, I had friends among the nurses, medical students and student nurses. All were kind and some of them came to see me daily. But that Sunday for some reason no one came. The following day, Monday, Nurse Ochi would certainly come at noon, but for some reason she did not either. I thought she must be on an emergency case.

Then a girl who worked in the laboratory came in rather quietly. I used to call her 'the French beauty queen', but in addition to being beautiful she was really kind-hearted. She sat down sadly on a chair.

'Hotta-san.'

With deliberate cheerfulness I asked, 'What's the matter? Doesn't he love you any more?'

'Why, Hotta-san, don't you know yet about Nishimura-sensei?'

That was enough to let me know that he had died. I was so overcome I forgot I was in hospital and I cried aloud like a child. There were three others in the room, all seriously ill, and the girl did not know what to do. I could only grieve.

I looked at the photo of Nishimura-sensei which I was using as a bookmark. In October of the previous year when I asked him for a photo, he had made a special visit to the photographer to have one taken. When he gave it to me he remarked, 'My wife says it looks like a photo of a dead person and she doesn't like it. I must look ill if she can say that. If you don't like it either, I'll take it back and get another.'

I was grateful to him for having it taken specially for me, when he was so busy. To be sure, it was not a good photo, but I was glad to have it.

Two months later he gave me a Christmas present, and as he left he said, 'If there's anything you want you mustn't hesitate to tell me.'

'Well, there is something,' I said. 'I would love to have some broiled salmon.'

When we had first met I had been so obstinate I had refused to accept anything, and now I could say this quite naturally.

'That's easy enough,' he answered.

On New Year's Eve in the evening he made a special journey to bring a tray of New Year's Eve delicacies which his wife had so kindly prepared. There was warm broiled salmon, fish and vegetables in soya sauce, black soy beans, and herring roe carefully arranged. It was all served separately for me and the others in the room. For the first time in my life I was away from home, ill and destitute, and I had no words to thank this couple who had given me this heart-warming New Year's food. It is hard enough to care for one's own relatives if they are ill for a long time, so I was literally unable to thank them for the wonderful love they had shown towards an unknown stranger.

But now that only led to more grief. In my mind I saw again the last time he had said goodbye and I wrote a poem on a scrap of paper:

> You replace the quilt which is slipping
>> off my bed, and go home.
> It is the last time.

I asked the nurse to place this poem and several others in the coffin.

The wake ended and also the funeral. When I heard there were over eight hundred at the funeral, many of them in tears, I could not help reflecting afresh on what a true Christian he was, loved by so many people.

Nurse Ochi explained, 'I couldn't tell you about him. His wife asked that you alone should not be told.'

I was deeply touched that his wife in the midst of her own grief had time to think of me lying ill.

Soon the autumn shadows deepened, and his widow cooked rice and mushrooms, made *misō* soup and brought me some. One glimpse of her face and I buried my head in the quilt, crying. Someone in the Kyoto area had heard of Nishimura-sensei's life and had sent the mushrooms, but I was too upset to appreciate them.

The Lonely Way

37

WITH NISHIMURA-SENSEI'S DEATH, Sapporo suddenly became empty for me. At that point Tadashi Maekawa came from Asahikawa for his check-up. It was his first visit since the operation. He had regained his previous weight and seemed well. They said they could find nothing wrong, and the operation was a success.

As my health insurance had come to an end we discussed whether I should go home or go to the Sapporo City Sanatorium. He thought for a while and said, 'If you can, come back to Asahikawa. Sapporo is so far away. It doesn't take long to get to your home, but it takes four or five hours to Sapporo.'

I had no desire to stay in Sapporo now that Nishimura-sensei had died, and to be in Asahikawa and see Tadashi Maekawa frequently would be much better. It would be difficult to return in my plaster cast, but with my brothers to help it was possible. I decided to return to Asahikawa immediately. He drew a long breath and said, 'I'll be waiting for you then,' and left.

Once I had decided to go home I wanted to go as soon as possible. I wrote to my family and they agreed, and my older brother Toshio and two younger brothers Tetsuo and Akio came to fetch me.

I finally left the hospital on October 26th, with a send-off from nurses, orderlies and patients. They moved me into the car in my plaster cast, my brothers crouching over me as if to cover me. I was returning to Asahikawa after twenty months. We passed through the Sapporo avenues of trees, now almost leafless, and on arrival at the station my elder brother carried me along the platform. It was a luxury, but they took two first class seats and laid me down with my cast on a plank between them.

At that point my younger brother Tetsuo arrived with my luggage, laughing, 'Oh dear, oh dear! I'm so embarrassed. Something slipped out of my hand and fell on to the platform with a clatter — the lid of the bed pan! Everyone burst out laughing.'

Tetsuo roared with laughter. The plastic *furoshiki* around it had come loose. But I could not forgive myself for embarrassing him.

As the time came to leave, the loudspeaker music blared out across the platform. Thinking of the people of Sapporo who had helped me, and of the death of Nishimura-sensei, I left praying silently.

I could see nothing, as I was lying down, but Akio sometimes told me what we were passing and then with my mirror I managed to look out of the window. How anyone could make such a journey was a wonder to me. But I was not unhappy. I had gone to Sapporo sitting up properly in a train and I was returning home on my back, but it did not distress me.

'I'm going back as a Christian. That's the wonderful thing. Now I've begun a new life.' And then, 'Tadashi-san, I'm coming to you, and I'm coming back as one who trusts in the same God as you do.'

The thought kept on coming back. I would see him often in Asahikawa. He would probably return to college in the spring and in five years' time I might be well again. If so, one day we could marry and have the joy of making a Christian home. Swayed by the movement of the train I dreamed about the future. But who can ever know what the future holds?

38

My sixth brother Haruo had stayed up all night repapering my room a soft cream. When I saw it again after twenty months' absence it was so light I scarcely recognised it. The mattress had been spread over a brand-new straw palliasse and snow-white sheets awaited me.

I had had tuberculosis for eight years now and caused so much financial trouble and worry, yet in spite of this my parents and family had gone to all this trouble to welcome me. During those eight years Haruo had moved from middle school to high school and now worked in a bank, and my youngest brother who had been in junior school was about to leave high school.

Moreover, during those eight years I had been in hospital five times. What a financial burden that must have been for my family! Even though I had now left hospital I had no idea how many years I would have to spend at complete rest in a plaster cast. My mother, who was over sixty, was taking responsibility for caring for me single-handed, for everything from eating and drinking to using the bed pan. I was both disabled and ill and yet my parents were even kinder to me than before.

Tadashi Maekawa arrived the very next day.

'I set off yesterday to meet you at the station, but on the way I changed my mind.'

Maybe he could not bear to see me carried clumsily on my elder brother's back. He had been considering my feelings. When my father saw me being carried out of the train just as I was in my padded dressing gown, his eyes had filled with tears and he said with difficulty, 'Welcome home. Welcome home.'

I was thirty-one. If I had been well I would probably have been married with a couple of children. What must my father have felt? We had no idea when I would be better. Tadashi Maekawa probably knew how my family would be feeling and I was glad he had not come to greet me.

'You must have found the train journey tiring.'

Tadashi-san's complexion, as he enquired so solicitously about me, was sallow. When he had visited Sapporo only a month earlier it had been different. He did not seem well. I was worried.

'Tadashi-san, something's the matter, isn't it?'

He smiled wanly. 'So you've noticed after all. I didn't want to worry anyone so I haven't told my father or mother . . . but recently I have been coughing up blood occasionally.'

I felt the warmth drain from my face. He was coughing up blood. It clearly indicated that the operation had failed. In spite of removing eight ribs the cavity had not healed. I found myself crying. He had faced the truth and handled it alone.

'Aya-chan, it's all right. You don't need to worry about it like that. It only means that there's some blood in the sputum, and now there's streptomycin and other new drugs.' He spoke cheerfully.

Previously he had come daily to visit me as he was less than six blocks away, and he had written to me daily without fail, but now his letters and visits were less frequent. He visited me three times in three weeks, but his face was as colourless as before. When I asked anxiously, 'Are you all right?' he would answer cheerfully, 'Fine, fine. I can go back to college next spring.'

39

I shall never forget November 16th. He had bought me the New Year gifts and cards which went on sale that day. Then, although it was so cold he made a special journey to the Health Centre to have my sputum tested, and as he returned on foot he called at the house again.

What did we talk about that day? Sadly men even forget the details of the things they discuss at final leave-taking, but

T–E

I remember him showing me several poems he had written after his operation.

> I took the rib they removed.
> It seemed transparent and pitiful.

Of the poems he showed me that day this was the most memorable because he then showed me the rib he had brought. I stared at it in silence as it lay on the straw mat, black with encrusted blood. As I have said he had endured the two painful operations partly for my sake, and although eagerly hoping for recovery was now coughing up blood again. It was too much and I could not even bear to look at it. Presently I spoke.

'Are you giving this to me?'

'Well, that's why I brought it, but you didn't look very interested so I was wondering whether to give up the idea.'

We both laughed that Japanese faces could be so expressionless. My face had been rigid with deep emotion, but he had thought I was not interested. Before long he placed his hands on the *tatami* mat and bowed courteously.

'Aya-chan, it's getting colder, I must go and rest for a while too. Next time it will be Christmas. Mind you don't catch cold.'

Then he stood up, and as he was about to leave he made two or three more remarks, bowed again as he stood there, made another remark, and having done this several times over finally burst out laughing.

'How many times have I bowed today? Actually I've been wanting to take your hand but couldn't bring myself to say so.'

As he said this he gently took my hand. We had been friends for five years and he still hesitated to take it, but having gripped it at last he seemed content. With one more *Sayonara!* he made a slight bow, and slid open the door.

'Oh, it's snowing hard. Shall I show you?'

He opened the doors wide and showed me the snow falling thick and fast in the garden. I could have gazed a long time at the scene reflected in my hand mirror, but he said gently, 'I'd better close them, it's cold.' He slid the doors quietly together again and left.

After that the occasional postcard came but he did not seem well. I was eagerly awaiting his promised Christmas visit, but in the end he never came then, either.

Three or four days after Christmas the January issue of *Araragi* arrived. I was astonished to see a postscript on selected poems. A member of *Araragi* had written about mine of November 1954:

> You replace the quilt which is slipping off my bed
> and go home.
> It is the last time.
>
> *Ayako Hotta*

> You replace the quilt which is slipping off my bed.
> Is it because you are drunk?
>
> *Tomi Sakamoto*

> The first is almost the same as the second. Are they both based on an original?

The editor agreed with the writer and deplored the similarity. Violent by nature, I literally blazed with anger. I could not sleep that night. The following day a card arrived from Tadashi Maekawa.

> I have been rather worried. These are the words of an ignorant writer. Please don't stop writing poetry because of this. I am sending an immediate protest to the publishers.

He must have written in haste. Unlike his usual postcards the characters were large and confused.

I wrote poems but I wrote them in one go. I rarely polished them and moreover I had hardly ever read an anthology. I preferred reading the novels of Mauriac and Dostoevsky to anthologies of poetry, and found that these gave me literary inspiration for poetry. In fact the *Araragi* magazine was the only book of poetry I read, and Tadashi Maekawa knew this better than anyone. Moreover, when I wrote poems I did not keep them carefully in an exercise book, but wrote them down haphazardly on scrap paper, on the backs of advertisements and anything else handy. He often scolded me for this and told me I should take better care of them. But I was content simply to write poetry. If he had not pressed me I would not have bothered sending contributions to *Araragi*. Because I was like this I soon forgot even my own poems, let alone remembering the poems of others. The accusation was even more regrettable because this poem had been written in tears, grieving for Nishimura-sensei's death. Immediately, I sent for my friend Rië and asked her to search through all the *Araragi* magazines in the house.

'See if you can find a similar poem and try not to miss anything.'

For several days she faithfully searched through all the volumes. A letter also came from Sakamoto-san of Kyoto saying that simply because these two poems were listed under the same title it did not follow that one had borrowed from the other.

The New Year came. I received sixteen pages of protest from Tadashi Maekawa addressed to the publishers and written on blank manuscript paper.

'Aya-chan, please look this over and send it on to the publishers.'

Even now I find it painful to recall that time. He was so weak then, that to write a single postcard exhausted him. When he had finished writing this letter he had had a lung haemorrhage. But nobody had told me how ill he was. I had no way of knowing he was confined to bed and could not get up for anything. Although he had explained he could not come at Christmas and said that his mother had written his New Year cards for him, I still did not realise how very ill he was. I thought he was probably being careful in the cold weather and that if he rested the bleeding would soon stop. If I had known he had written this protest from his death bed I would certainly have sent it to the publishers. As it was, I did not want anyone to defend me.

As I lay on my back I wrote to the editor. My letter and Sakamoto-san's were included in the March issue of *Araragi*. I quote from part of mine:

> As for the poem that was put in the coffin, I had no time to imitate anyone, but I'm sorry that you go as far as describing the poem I wrote in my grief for Nishimura-sensei as a fraud. I believe that Sakamoto-san of Kyoto probably wrote likewise from her own experience.
>
> I am undergoing total rest because of a tubercular spine, and there is also a cavity in my lungs. When the heavy winter quilt slipped down I had not the strength to straighten it. The ward orderlies and visitors always did this for me and there was nothing extraordinary about Nishimura-sensei doing the same. That day he did it as usual, but it was for the last time.
>
> Because we look to you as our teacher we trust in the poems that you choose for us. Please have more faith in those of us who trust you.
>
> January 6th

On receiving our letters the editor retracted his previous statement and explained further about the problem of similar poems. Finally he kindly wrote, 'At all events I'm glad to say that from what you have both written personally, I'm sure both of you were genuine and sincere.'

To be honest, when I read that January issue I was so angry that I was foolish enough to think I would write no more poetry. This was not surprising, since I was too inexperienced to be able to imagine the problems of the editor, but this incident was valuable for me. It gave me the opportunity of reconsidering my attitude in writing, and taught me to wrestle seriously with every single poem. Of course Tadashi Maekawa's letter also encouraged me: 'Don't let something like this stop you writing poetry.' If something like this could stop me then I ought certainly not

to have started in the first place. If I had withdrawn from
Araragi in a fit of anger I should really have lost a great deal.

Later I sent them this poem:

> To learn to write about ordinary things in an ordinary
> way
> is to live in reality.

The *Araragi* style of poetry drew out the truth about
mankind. In *Araragi* they lay stress on portraying nature. I
was told this meant reflecting life, and I adopted this attitude
when I wrote.

How often I still recall Tadashi Maekawa's deep concern
for me, not just for my faith but in urging me to write poetry.
His desire when he read the correspondence, that I should
not give up, affects me even more today. Occasionally he
would say,

'Aya-chan, if you ever give up poetry, whatever you do,
express yourself in some other kind of literature.'

Now I am writing novels, and what I learned from *Araragi*
has been most valuable. Of course if I had studied it more
faithfully my style would not be as poor as it is and I owe an
apology to my fellow-members in *Araragi* for this.

40

After he had written that protest for me, for some reason
Tadashi Maekawa's cards suddenly ceased and I did not
know why. I waited, wondering if he would pay me a surprise visit, but he never came. When the middle of January
passed, I grew increasingly uneasy.

Finally, at the end of January a sealed letter arrived,
written by his mother. He had had lung haemorrhages since
January 6th and had been unable to receive even his close
friends. If it was January 6th, it had happened right after
he had written the sixteen pages of protest. I wanted to get
up immediately and go to see him.

After that I occasionally had news of his condition from his mother, but I grew more and more apprehensive. If news came that he was a little better, then the next news was always of another haemorrhage and, as during his operation, I could do nothing but pray and berate myself for my own helplessness.

One day I saw a fly crossing my room. It was alive. It had survived the severe cold of Asahikawa and made me think of spring. Both Tadashi Maekawa and I, like that fly, had barely survived the winter. There was a lump in my throat. But by and by there were days when the stove was no longer lit and, before we knew it, it was April.

April 25th was my birthday. Each year he had never failed to give me a book for my birthday, and if he had been well he would have remembered to get me one this year. I was reading my Bible by myself and thinking of him and his repeated haemorrhages when suddenly an envelope arrived from him. Astonished and overjoyed I cut it open. It was written in pencil on white tissue-like paper.

For your birthday. I am always praying for you. Tadashi.

To Ayako, April 25th, 1954.

In November and December blood appeared in my sputum. On January 6th there was a real haemorrhage for the first time and since then blood-stained phlegm. I have a haemorrhage each week of 10 to 100 cc. My father, mother, or someone else stays up all night caring for me. As inhalations make it easier to bring up the sputum, my mother has to get up to me three or four times a night.

Apparently there is one weak blood vessel in the area operated on. If I haemorrhage at night we call a cousin who is a doctor. As this had not happened before, it was disconcerting at first, but on the whole I've got used to it. However I shall have to write what I want to say to you.

Please thank your mother for her visit, but please don't worry too much. My mother was feeling discouraged

when she went to the front door. I could not read your
letter, but I got the gist from her.

I'm sorry, I can't visit you for six months. Please pray
for me. At present the expense of streptomycin and other
drugs and the doctor's visits is heavy. I can't give you a
book. This is as much as I can do. My mother has helped
me. Get better soon.

I finished the letter and my heart was stricken. The pen-
cilled characters were confused, quite unlike his normal
methodical writing. Lying as he was, his mother steadying
the paper, he had poured his whole heart and soul into
writing that letter.

Never before had I received such a sincere yet desperate
birthday greeting as this. In spite of sorrow, I was deeply
moved. I re-read it three or four times. He had poured his
own life into writing it and I tried to put all I had into reading
it. With the final 'get better soon' I seemed to hear so many
of his words ringing in my ears.

'I'm sorry, I can't visit you for six months.' So he had
written, but I wondered fearfully whether after six months
he would ever be able to pick up a pen again. With the one
phrase 'get better soon' he evoked a flood of emotions. I
felt he had wanted to say, 'No matter what happens you're
going to get better.' I read it over and over again, wondering
whether this was simply a birthday letter or whether he was
tacitly saying goodbye.

41

Spring is a depressing time of year for tubercular patients,
for when the leaves begin to open they experience a physical
setback and wonder if the disease is breaking out again.

On May 1st my whole body felt as stiff as a board and I
also had a temperature. Although I was tired and it was night,
for some reason I could not sleep. I had finished reading
the Bible and praying as usual, but I was curiously alert.

I was wondering anxiously, 'If I'm unwell like this, is Tadashi-san unwell too?' when the clock struck midnight. Then his face flashed before my eyes again and again like a sign — his face when we first met at the sanatorium and he removed his mask; his stern face when he forbade me to drink *saké*; his happy face as he chaired a poetry contest; his touching face when he struck his foot on Shunkodai Hill. Very clearly but steadily they followed one after the other like the scenes of a film. I was not recalling them voluntarily. In a mysterious way, I felt someone was showing them to me, whether I willed it or not. Trying to regain my composure and shake off the feeling, I looked at my watch. It was already past one a.m. I felt very tired and sank into a deep sleep.

The following day, May 2nd, I had a temperature all morning and was out of sorts. It puzzled me that Tadashi Maekawa's face had drifted past again and again during the night. Why should I have seen him like that for over an hour when I made no effort to do so? As I pondered it, the defence force planes were flying over the house continually. It was a terrible noise for someone as ill as I was. I wondered if the noise was tormenting him too.

As evening drew near my older sister came in quietly to see me, wearing a black dress.

'How are you, Aya-chan?'

For my sister she was extraordinarily quiet. I asked moodily, 'What's the matter, Yuri-san? Are you off to a wake somewhere?'

'No.' And she just went out again.

I thought she had gone off at once because I was under the weather. She brought my evening meal in but I had no appetite. I just picked at the side dishes and then had it removed.

Not long after the evening meal she returned with my father. He began to speak hesitantly, 'Ayako, I know you feel things very keenly . . .'

I listened indifferently, thinking he was concerned because I had been unwell all day. How dense one can be!

'Ayako, I have come to inform you about Tadashi Maekawa.'

My father did not normally say, 'I have come to inform you'. At last I realised something was wrong and as he began to speak again I tore the words from his mouth and cried, 'Has he died?'

Even I was surprised at the strength of my own voice. My sister covered her face.

'When?'

'At one fourteen early this morning.'

In a flash I remembered those visions of his face. However I tried to stop them I could not. Maybe those drifting visions were his final farewell and I was realising this for the first time.

'He's died?' Suddenly violent anger welled up. Yes, it was undoubtedly anger rather than sorrow. Would there ever be another young man as genuine as Tadashi Maekawa? I was overcome with uncontrollable anger against the One who had snatched life away from so true a person.

'Yuri-san, please bring me the scissors.'

'Scissors?' My sister looked at me doubtfully.

'Yes, please bring them.'

I took them from her and cut off the front of my hair. She watched me quietly. Wrapping my hair and a photo of myself in writing paper I gave them to her.

'Yuri-san, you'll go to the wake for me? Would you put this in the coffin?' I was angry, but somehow I was getting control of myself.

'Aya-chan, that's a lovely thing to do.' She seemed relieved and told me about his death.

About seven-thirty p.m. the previous night Tadashi San had become unconscious during the evening meal and had died without regaining consciousness. My sister had already visited his home. She said his mother was so distressed she was now in bed. Then she went on, 'It was decided not to tell you in case you couldn't stand it, but I was against this. I thought you might learn about him from someone's letter and then you would certainly have wished we'd told you.

When you asked me if I was going to someone's wake I didn't know what to say.'

Everyone could see Tadashi Maekawa was vital to me, so it was not surprising they feared I would take the news badly. My timid younger brother could not bear the thought of my knowing, and had been out of the house all day. But for some reason I did not have a heart attack, nor did I faint. I just felt unspeakably angry that someone like me should live and someone as fine as he should die.

The evening wore on and at last I began to realise he had really died. Every evening at nine o'clock I used to pray, and I had prayed earnestly that he would be healed as soon as possible. But from that night I could never pray for his recovery any more, and at that thought I burst out crying.

The flood of tears did not stop easily. Lying on my back, the tears trickled down my neck and soaked my hair behind my ears. Imprisoned in a plaster cast, I could not give way to grief, though sick at heart, nor could I find relief by walking around. I could only lie and gaze at the ceiling and cry.

I did not sleep at all that night. At one fourteen in the morning, the time of his death, I was crying bitterly. I could not but grieve that his face had flashed before me again and again the previous night and I had known nothing of his dying. I had never dreamt he would die just one week after sending that birthday letter, so even those visionary glimpses of him, even my sister's mourning, had not prepared me for the possibility.

The next day was fine. My father, sister and nephews went to the funeral. My home and his were less than half a mile apart and I desperately wanted to go with them in a taxi, or somehow. If only I could have one glimpse of his face for the last time, to bid him farewell. But that would have been sheer self-indulgence. I needed total rest in bed and I could not possibly mention it.

42

One night, a few days later, there was the sound of breathing nearby. As I slept by myself in a separate room I could not hear anybody else asleep, but I heard that breathing very clearly.

'It's Tadashi-san,' I thought.

At first the unexpected sound beside me was uncanny, but when I was convinced that it was he it was very comforting: 'He's sleeping beside me.' Although he had died physically his spirit had not ceased to exist. I cried as I listened to the sound of breathing, and as I wept I was comforted.

The mysterious sound continued for ten nights and then stopped abruptly. I listened intently but it could no longer be heard. For the second time indescribable desolation engulfed me. I seemed to be totally alone. He was no longer bound to this earth, but after death he had slept by my side for ten days. Even now I sometimes recall that strange breathing.

At that point I began to think about Heaven. In July of the previous year I had lost my dear and respected teacher Nishimura, and less than a year later my beloved Tadashi Maekawa had been called away. At that time Heaven was dearer than this earth.

Every few days I had a bad day when the tears could not be checked. Yasuhiko Mafuji, on hearing of Tadashi-san's death, came from Sapporo to see me. I told my mother I would not see him, but she brought him to my room saying he had come specially.

'I didn't want to see you,' I announced.

He looked at me, taken aback. 'I'm sorry. I only thought of my own feelings. I was forgetting you wouldn't want to meet people.'

What did we talk about? I only remember saying, 'Don't!' when the subject of Tadashi Maekawa was touched on.

After that many friends called to console me, but I didn't

want to hear his name on anyone else's lips. Who was able to weep with me? His life with them and his life with me were two totally different things, and when people tried to praise him or mourn for him it was no more than empty words to me. Finally I decided to see no one for a while and grieve for him alone.

I had been eagerly awaiting a visit from his mother and a month after his death she called. We looked at each other and burst into tears. Being his mother she was the only person in the world who could weep with me. She brought me as mementos his padded gown, his writings, his last wishes, his diaries and poems, and she also brought me over six hundred letters which I had written to him. These letters were numbered in chronological order and neatly arranged in numerous boxes, revealing how precious they had been to him.

Among his final instructions there was a reference to me in a note to his parents: 'About Aya-chan — as you probably know, I have done nothing to be ashamed of.' He wanted his parents to know there had been no physical relationship between us.

As he had written his last words to me before his condition grew too serious he had formally put his seal on the envelope.

Aya-chan, I'm so grateful for the wonderfully real friendship we have had together. You have truly been the first and last person in my life. Aya-chan, even though I die, you have surely promised not to give up living or to become negative. If by any chance you were to break this promise, then my confidence in you would have been misplaced, but you are not like that!

I have mentioned this once and I hesitate to repeat it, but I have never asked to be the only person in your life and I want to say so once more. Life is hard and perplexing. If you were compelled to live an unnatural life because of an old promise, that would be the saddest thing of all.

I have never discussed you in detail with anyone and I am returning to you the bundles of your letters, my diaries (which have references to you) and my poems. No one else will know what I have thought, and nothing concerning our relationship can fall into other people's hands. In the end, rumours apart, there is no evidence which others can use to bind you. You can start with a perfectly 'clean sheet', and be free of me. When debts are settled on the final day, what you have said to me will leave no mark. You are free of all restrictions and this is my last gift to you. I have written this early, just in case . . .

> February 12th, 1954, Tadashi.
> To Ayako-san

What deep concern this last note revealed. His greatest anxiety was for my life after his death. His main worry was lest I commit suicide. But he was also concerned lest another man appear in my life and I would not feel able to act freely because I was chained to my past with him. So he sent me his diaries and the letters and poems, so that I could dispose of them as I wished.

But how could I burn the record of such a precious relationship? Far from burning them, instead I wrote each thought of him in a poem and published them in *Araragi* and elsewhere:

When I watch a cloud drifting across the sky in May
It is hard to believe you have died.

Must I go on living in a plaster cast
When each day is desolate, now you are dead?

I am increasingly lonely since your death.
This morning the first cuckoo[1] called.

[1] The cry of the cuckoo evokes feelings of sadness and melancholy for the Japanese.

When I found the toothpick stuck in the padded
   gown you left me,
I could not withhold my tears.

I wiped away the tears that ran past my ears
And fresh tears came.

I open my eyes in the darkness,
Wondering if you might possibly appear to me,
   though dead.

Clasping the small *paulownia*[2] box which holds your
   bone and my hair,
I slept.

In a dream I saw the coffin they had described,
Covered with fresh marguerites.

I live grieving for your death.
Oh, that my life might also be short!

I came to know you at the end of much suffering,
and now you have died after five brief years.

You lived according to Christian teaching and died
   chaste.
You were thirty-five.

You were more gentle than a woman,
But you kept to your convictions.

When you found me smoking and turned sadly away,
I was attracted to you.

From our first meeting until the end you never
   changed.

[2] Wood of a Chinese tree with heart-shaped leaves and lavender-blue
flowers.

You were courteous and gentle.

Among your dying wishes you mentioned a telegram
    requesting an autopsy.
You were a medical student.

Even in my dream you were dead.
I clasped your lifeless body and I died too.

You taught me about original sin,
And I remember your intense eyes.

The mountain dove sang on the hill in the evening
And we knelt and prayed to Jesus together.

You held me in your arms as if I were your wife.
Oh, come back, come back from Heaven.

These laments arose one after the other, but one of his
friends, a university lecturer, wrote this in *Araragi* and then
gave up writing poetry once and for all:

My teacher was neither Mokichi nor Bunmei.[3]
He was Tadashi Maekawa who was ill for ten years.

Another who had published some good poems in *Araragi*
also gave up after Tadashi Maekawa's death. Curiously,
they each said, 'I can't write any more, now that Tadashi-san
has died.'

As I wrote poem after poem I thought about this, wondering if these two loved him more than I did.

Tadashi Maekawa had to die at thirty-five years of age,
but I wondered what he would actually have done if he had
lived. Sometimes my own bruised heart was urged on by the
thought that I must now live his life for him.

[3] Saito Mokichi, 1882–1953, a founder and editor of *Araragi* and one
of the greatest *tanka* poets. Tsuchiya Bunmei, 1891–, then editor of
Araragi.

'Tadashi-san wanted to get better — I must get better. He wanted to write poetry — I must write poetry. He wanted to go to church — I must go to church.' I decided to make his will mine and simply live as he had wanted to do.

But without his affection, I could only weep. I could not sleep at night until one fourteen a.m., the hour of his death had passed. I could not help feeling that if I were not awake at this time he might be lonely.[4] I was tempted to feel I wanted to die at that same hour. I had decided I would live and yet I wanted after all to die.

On one such day several letters arrived for me from strangers.

[4] Many Japanese feel keenly the possible loneliness of the spirits of the dead who are now cut off from the family, and a great deal of the prayer offered at graves and the family Buddhist shrines today arises from this desire to reassure the dead that they are remembered.

A Way Prepared

43

THE LETTERS WERE from tubercular patients living all over Japan. I opened the envelopes wondering what it was all about, and then I knew. Shortly before Tadashi Maekawa died I had written to a magazine for the sick, offering to send free copies of *Voice* to patients. This was a monthly magazine presided over by the pastor of Hayama church, and Tadashi Maekawa had sent it to me each month. It was a slim Christian periodical of under twenty pages, but I drank in the contents and they never ceased to inspire me.

I could not go to church while I was ill and I envied those healthy people who could go and hear such preaching every week. Lying motionless by myself, there were times when I longed to hear some teaching from the Bible. My longing was so great, I thought how wonderful it would be if some pastor, passing by, might call in to see me. At such times I re-read this pastor's writings.

But one day it suddenly occurred to me that there must be many people like myself throughout the country who would love to hear such teaching. If I sent *Voice* to those people they would be delighted. As I received free copies, I could send them free of charge, and I said as much in a letter to the magazine. Before long the letter was published and patients who saw it were writing to me from all quarters.

God had already prepared something for me to do, at a time when I could do nothing but grieve for Tadashi Maekawa. I wrote a card to each person and sent them the magazine. But I received so many letters that in no time at all the copies I had to hand were exhausted.

I still had to write as I lay flat in the plaster cast. After Tadashi Maekawa's death I grew even weaker and was so tired after writing one card that I could do nothing else for a day or two; but, praying for help, I answered each letter I received and ordered back numbers from the pastor.

More and more letters came from the readers and there were many who were far more wretched than I was. As a result of tubercular joints there were people who could neither kneel nor sit. They could only stand or lie down. One mother who had been ill for a long time had been abandoned by her husband and even estranged from her own child. While one wife was ill, her husband took another woman into the house and the wife had to eat meals prepared by the other woman. One student had a foot amputated for tubercular arthritis and then developed spinal tuberculosis, and now this had spread to a kidney and he was in hospital to have the kidney removed. Whoever they were, all these people in the midst of their truly tragic circumstances believed in God and were facing life with courage.

Compared with such people, life was almost too kind to me. Hadn't I parents, brothers and sisters, and a separate room of my own? Tadashi Maekawa's death was tragic, but it was a simple grief compared with the humiliation of eating meals prepared by one's husband's mistress. Naturally, when I wrote back I tried to encourage them.

Once again letters of thanks arrived one after another from these people. I was astonished. It had never entered my head as I lay alone and ill in far-away Asahikawa that any letter or postcard of mine could bring such pleasure and comfort to others. So I made many friends all over the country, and among them were some who were searching for the truth. Letters came earnestly enquiring about Christianity, and I knew so little.

This thought gave me a reason for living. It was these people who really sustained me as I wept for Tadashi Maekawa, and in this way I discovered in my own experience the simple truth that as I comforted others I was comforted myself, and as I encouraged others I myself was encouraged; until I found that at some point, without my being aware of it, I had been drawn out of my grief and was able to write like this:

> Day by day I lie, recalling the names of my
> sick friends, one by one,
> And praying for them.

At the same time I at last began to realise how rebellious my own faith had been. I believed in God, or rather I thought I did, but what did 'believing' really mean in my case? I had been very angry when Tadashi Maekawa had died and afterwards I had often complained, 'God, why did you call Tadashi-san without taking my life too?' or 'God, wouldn't a wonderful person like Tadashi-san still have been of use in this world? Wouldn't it have been better for him to live instead of a worthless person like me?'

I had openly voiced my dissatisfaction to God and had gone on complaining to Him. But I did not stop believing in Him. I never felt there was no God after all, and the fact that I turned round and complained to Him, demonstrated this. But then I realised my attitude was wrong.

In the Bible it says, 'God is love'. Human beings like myself cannot really understand His ways, but I came to see that if God is love, then Tadashi Maekawa's death came at the time when God intended it and was certainly the best thing for him. I saw too that because God is righteous He does what is right. Because He is good He does what is good. Even though I could not understand it, human as I was, some day I certainly would. As I confessed, 'O God, all that You have done is good,' all my complaints and grudging discontent ended. I tried then to accept everything He had done.

With such an attitude I went on corresponding with sick people all over the country, and before long even made friends with a prisoner under the death sentence.

At the same time there was a sick man in Sapporo with whom I was corresponding. He had once worked in a bank, but had been ill for nearly ten years. Although he was wasted by TB he edited the Christian magazine *Figtree* by himself, and cut the stencils himself on his hospital bed. He was a person of character who had not only learnt how to cut stencils through a correspondence course but had won a government award and afterwards been invited to lecture on printing and copying.

In this magazine *Figtree*, the sick, the condemned, and also pastors and evangelists contributed their thoughts and news. Here were exposed men's individual lives and joys and sorrows, and it seemed as if whatever faith people had was vividly revealed.

In February 1956, a letter appeared in *Figtree* for the first time from someone called Mitsuyo who like me, lived in Asahikawa. Since the letter seemed mainly to contain news of condemned prisoners I felt quite certain that he also was a condemned man. Mitsuyo was certainly a good name. There is a verse in the Bible 'You are the light of the world'. Probably his parents had taken the characters for Light and World from the Bible verse and called him Mitsuyo. And yet this made me grieve as I secretly wondered how he had become a convict.

I thought I was the only subscriber to *Figtree* in Asahikawa at that time, so the advent of this person Mitsuyo Miura attracted my attention. My home was only 200 yards from the prison. I assumed he must be living inside that high wall. While I was wondering whether to write to him, the next issue of *Figtree* arrived. It contained a brief letter from him.

Ayako Hotta, I don't know where you live, although we are both in Asahikawa, but please go on writing; and take care of yourself.

I was convinced it, too, came from a criminal.

44

Soon it would be May again, the month Tadashi Maekawa died. This time last year he had still been alive. If I had known that he was going to die so soon I would have written to him daily, however hard it was for me. Now I spent each day going over and over this in my mind. Then it was my own birthday, on April 25th, and the letter that Tadashi-san had sent every year no longer came. Remembering the one he had sent from his death bed, I spent most of the day crying. However many birthdays came around in future, there would never be another letter from him. The thought made my life suddenly empty. I was already thirty-three. Ill as I was, I could roughly guess at what lay ahead. I too would get worse and die, or else recover only to grow old alone.

I had hardly seen anyone while I mourned for Tadashi Maekawa and maybe this had made me more lonely. I could not help feeling that if I died now, there would be little in my present existence to regret losing. I knew of the tragic lives of many of my sick friends, but was still apt to let my own grief prostrate me. What a blessing if would be if I could die on the first anniversary of his death.

Suddenly I realised how I was thinking. It appalled me. Wasn't I supposed to be living as Tadashi Maekawa had wanted to? If I had taken over his life, shouldn't I be living it with determination? Shouldn't I expect to get well again, along with the other sick friends God had given me? I pulled myself up. Nothing would come from being engrossed in my own grief. No, my own life was withering away. Once the period of mourning ended on May 2nd, I decided to receive all those who came to visit me. For a whole year I had never slept before one fourteen a.m., the time when he died. This was wrong and at last I knew it.

Life is indeed a strange thing. It certainly does not work out as expected. Suddenly something quite unforeseen happens. Unknown callers began to surge in like a flood, one after another. A medical student from Hokudai University, a poet and fellow patients were among them. I still think it amazing, the way they appeared as if they had been waiting for the end of mourning. I was no more than an unknown invalid, but they read my poems, knew my name, came to see me, and became my greatest friends as I lay there immobile.

From that time my room never lacked visitors. Sometimes there were three or even four in one hour, and on a full day seven or eight. Every day my mother was busy welcoming them. At rare intervals there was a day when no one came, and then she would remark in a disappointed way. 'I wonder what has happened today?' Some would talk for two or three hours, and when they left others arrived within ten minutes. On other days I was never without a visitor.

June 18th was one such day I will never forget. It was a beautiful Saturday afternoon. My mother came in holding a postcard.

'Someone called Miura has come to see you.'

Momentarily I caught my breath and thought, 'Miura the criminal! Why?' Quickly I scanned the card. It was from the editor of *Figtree* to Mitsuyo Miura. He gave him my address and asked him to visit me if he had time. He did not seem to be a criminal after all! If not, then did he work in the prison? Otherwise he would not have known so much about the prisoners. It was strange that I had been so convinced he was a criminal. Actually he had corresponded with them and tried to help and encourage them.

But the editor had also made a mistake. Seeing the note from Miura in *Figtree*, 'Ayako Hotta, I don't know where you live, although we are both in Asahikawa,' he jumped to the conclusion that Mitsuyo Miura was a woman, immediately sent him my address, and casually asked him to visit me.

When Mitsuyo Miura saw the card he was a little embarrassed but, after thinking it over for a few days, he decided to come and visit me. Of course I learned all this later, and I thank his parents from my heart for giving him a name which could be confused with a woman's. If he had been called Mitsuo, the editor might never have written that postcard and my present life would then have been quite different.

My mother showed him to my room. There was the sound of soft footsteps crossing the passage and a young man in a very light grey suit came in. Catching sight of him I was startled. How closely he resembled the dead Tadashi Maekawa!

As we introduced ourselves, even his quiet voice was like Tadashi-san's. I stared in amazement at each feature of his face, thinking, 'You're so alike, you're so alike.'

I had gradually regained strength, once I began meeting people again, and that day I had found I could sit up. When I told him about this he was as delighted for me as if it had been for himself.

He told me that fourteen years earlier he had undergone surgery for a tubercular kidney and the remaining one was also infected, but thanks to antibiotics he had completely recovered.

'When I was in pain and could not sleep on my side, I spent the night sitting propped up on pillows. That is what I was like then, and now I am able to work. Don't give up!'

In every way he was so like Tadashi Maekawa that I felt I was dreaming. I enquired, 'Where do you work?' thinking it would be the prison, but contrary to my expectations he replied, 'In the Asahikawa Forestry office.'

Forestry! My heart leapt. The Forestry Department was only 300 yards from my home. Did he pass us daily on his way to and from work? I was ill-mannered enough to blurt out, 'Are you still single?'

He was. He looked about twenty-seven or twenty-eight, five or six years younger than I was. I wondered whether he had a girl friend.

But I asked him, 'Will you read me one of your favourite Bible passages, please?'

Without hesitation he read Christ's words from John's Gospel Chapter 14:

'Let not your heart be troubled;
believe in God, believe also in me.
In my Father's house are many rooms;
if it were not so would I have told you
that I go to prepare a place for you?
And when I go and prepare a place for you,
I will come again and take you to myself,
that where I am you may be also.'

From his choice I knew that he was looking forward to
Heaven. Then I went on, and asked him what hymns he
liked. Immediately he sang:

Oh, Lord, I want to draw nearer to you,
Even if the upward road lies through the cross,
Why should I grieve?
Oh, Lord, I want to draw nearer to you.[1]

His voice was beautiful, it seemed to have been made for
singing hymns.

That night I wrote immediately to thank him and invited
him to come again, but no answer or visit came. Bleakly I
wondered whether he had come once, merely out of duty,
because the editor requested it. Then a strange thought
occurred to me. Supposing he were not human? Maybe
God had secretly taken pity on me because I had longed for
Tadashi Maekawa so much, and had sent someone very like
him. His close resemblance to Tadashi-san had made such a
clear impression upon me, it was scarcely surprising that
my thoughts took this turn.

45

For what seemed a very long time there was neither word
nor visit from Mitsuyo Miura, though I see from his diary
that he came the second time on the evening of July 3rd. I
was awaiting it so impatiently that it felt like the beginning
of August to me.

[1] *Nearer my God to Thee.*

One day my father hurried into my room. 'Ayako, Maekawa-san's younger brother has come to see you.' But the person who was shown in was not Tadashi Maekawa's younger brother. It was Mitsuyo Miura.

There were other similar incidents. When Mitsuyo Miura first attended the Asahikawa *Araragi* meeting later on, everyone was startled by someone greeting him with, 'Maekawa-san! We haven't seen you for ages.' For a moment they seemed to think he should have known of Tadashi Maekawa's death, but he was probably mistaking him for Tadashi-san's younger brother.

Moreover, one day one of my pupils came to visit me. Seeing Tadashi Maekawa's photograph by my bed he exclaimed in surprise, 'Hotta-san, do you know Miura-san?' He and Mitsuyo Miura attended the same church. Although he was told it was someone quite different he looked very unconvinced and said over and over again, 'It's him exactly, it's just like Miura-san.'

Even in his interests and thinking, Mitsuyo Miura closely resembled Tadashi Maekawa. Since he wrote poetry I lent him the *Araragi* magazine and encouraged him to join. He listened with interest and said he would try going to the Asahikawa meetings.

That day he left after twenty or thirty minutes, but I felt my heart had been rocked to its foundations. I began to realise I must watch myself.

On August 24th, he came for the third time. The reflection of the summer sun on the verandah was blinding. As he left he prayed for me, 'O God, I don't mind if you give her my life, but please make her well again.'

I was deeply moved by his prayer. No one had ever prayed such a thing for me before and, as yet, neither had I ever offered my life for someone else's. I had been able to sympathise with people and think 'Poor thing, I wish I could bear her sufferings for her', but I could not pray 'O God, I'll bear her suffering, so please release her'. Everyone holds themselves dear, and prayer is a serious matter to those who believe in God. Supposing the prayer is answered? Who can deliberately go to such lengths? For the believer, thinking and praying may appear to be the same thing, but actually they are quite different. It is no easy thing to have the sincerity and love needed to pray 'You can take my life'. But Miura-san had made that difficult request in all sincerity and when he had only met me three times at that.

So I was moved, and in the emotion of the moment I stretched out my hand spontaneously and he gripped it firmly. His hand was muscular and warm. I learned later that this was the first time he had ever shaken hands with someone of the opposite sex!

After this he came two or three times a month and we exchanged letters. But as autumn drew to a close my temperature returned, with night sweats. When I talked, my sputum became more blood-stained and once again I could not receive visitors.

Tonight the atmosphere of my room is deathly
As I cough up blood and conceal it from my parents.

One day when I was still without visitors my mother brought me some fruit and a letter from him.

'Miura-san sends his greetings,' she said.

'Has he gone already?'

'Yes, he just sent you his greetings and left.'

I was desolate. Although he had come to the door I had been unable to see him and it made me feel utterly bereft. In the letter he had written in beautiful characters, 'I'm praying for you. Please, please take care of yourself,' and he had enclosed five thousand *yen*.[2] That was a lot of money to me. I read this letter over and over, but however many times I did so, it said no more than that he was praying and I must take care of myself. I put it by my pillow and thought about him.

I now had many male friends — about as many as I had had when I first met Tadashi Maekawa. The only difference was that, now I was a Christian, those who had been coming

2 £5 or US $12·50.

to see me were serious and kind-hearted and a few had even become fond of me. Some already had sweethearts and were distressed when they were attracted to me. Some were coming daily, some every three days or so, some once a week. My room was busy.

But among them Mitsuyo Miura alone was different. At the front door he would always enquire how I was from my mother and say, 'If she's not so well I won't come in.' And if he came in he only stayed a short time. Although I wanted him to stay longer he would read the Bible, sing a hymn, discuss poetry a little and pray, and then go home. He was so concerned for my health.

Now that such visits had ended, I thought all this over again as I read his letters. How very faithful he was! He seemed a rather rare sort of person, and I told myself to keep him at a distance. Yet I could not forget the fact that he resembled Tadashi Maekawa. Nor could I deny that I was attracted to Mitsuyo Miura. But if this was because he so closely resembled the dead Tadashi-san then I was ignoring Mitsuyo Miura himself. However much they looked alike, had the same faith and shared the same interests, they were two different people. I had no intention of treating Mitsuyo Miura as a substitute for Tadashi Maekawa but, all the same, the fact that he resembled my dead friend was a comfort to me, and this made me cautious.

Before long it was Christmas again. I recalled the previous Christmas. I had welcomed it, lying alone in this room helpless. The photos of my many friends were arranged on the bookstand and I had had a chair placed by my bed — for Jesus. I remembered the many Christmases I had spent with Tadashi Maekawa. He and Nishimura-sensei had lost their health and been called to Heaven, and I had nothing but a solitary Christmas to look forward to. Nevertheless, as I read my Bible and silently sang a hymn, this Christmas all alone had become a foretaste of Heaven to me. In spite of losing my health, my lover and my teacher, I had suddenly been filled with a deep and overwhelming joy.

Surely Jesus Christ had sat on that empty chair. Even

now when I think about it I feel that I have never had such a wonderfully rich Christmas as that year. God Himself was with me and the words of the Bible had proved true:

> 'My grace is sufficient for you,
> for my power is made perfect in weakness.'[3]

Thinking of that experience I tried to welcome the present Christmas, alone again. As before, a chair was by my bed and my friends' photographs were arranged on the book-stand. It was going to be exactly the same as last year.

But for some reason I did not find comfort. Deep inside I was constantly hoping Mitsuyo Miura would come. It was different from last Christmas when I had been waiting for God alone because there was no one else.

Mitsuyo Miura called that evening. Would my mother encourage him to come in? Suddenly he appeared and I was so happy that tears came to my eyes. He explained that he had been so busy doing the Forestry Department accounts, he had not even been able to go to church. And he gave me a fountain pen, apologising because it was not new. Probably he had not even had time to go shopping in the town. He prayed with me briefly and immediately returned to the office.

I was delighted to have the fountain pen he had used. It was far better than a new one. As I thought of him holding it as he wrote his diary and letters, this pen which knew his inner secrets was very dear to me. Now I could scarcely say I had spent Christmas alone. Over and over again I removed the cap and gazed at it, holding it up to the light. Then I wrote in my diary.

This was just the way someone in love would behave — and my heart sank at the thought. Far from forgetting Tadashi Maekawa, I was constantly thinking of him. Yet in spite of this I was being attracted to another man and I hated myself for being so fickle.

[3] 2 Corinthians 12: 9.

46

We had welcomed the New Year, and before long the warm March winds came to melt the snow. Gradually I got better, the temperature and sputum disappeared, and once again friends could come and see me. I was finding it extremely disturbing to be single and unattached. In fact, that I had no ties to anyone actually frightened me. I had been more settled when everyone had looked on me as Tadashi Maekawa's girl friend.

'But now I'm free to love anyone,' I told myself. 'Even though I'm sick I have friends who are fond of me. No one would reproach me for loving one of them. But am I really free?'

Wanting to remain loyal to Tadashi Maekawa all my life, I was finding myself too full of human frailty. It was true that I had loved him and had been loved in return and now I felt I loved him even more, yet my heart was so drawn to Mitsuyo Miura. No, I was not free.

That evening Mitsuyo Miura arrived. As soon as we had exchanged greetings he announced, 'Hotta-san, I'm going to be transferred.'

He seemed delighted, but as I took in his news I felt the blood drain from my face. On seeing this he hastened to explain.

'When I say transferred, it's only to the Kagura Cho office.'

I breathed a sigh of relief. He could commute to Kagura Cho from home!

After he had gone I wondered why everything had gone black before my eyes at the mention of his transfer. Did I really love him after all? But this was how I had loved Tadashi-san. Then as I turned it over in my mind I recalled Tadashi Maekawa's last letter.

I have mentioned this once and I hesitate to repeat it,

but I have never asked to be the only person in your life and I want to say so once more. Life is hard and perplexing. If you were compelled to live an unnatural life because of an old promise, that would be the saddest thing of all.

How well he understood the human heart. At the time of his death the mature wisdom of his letter had not come home to me. I still did not know the full meaning of those words, 'life is hard and perplexing'. I was unsophisticated. I even imagined that such consideration for me was unnecessary. After all, I had enough self-confidence to think I could remain loyal to him all my life. So I was surprised at his concern for me, and far from knowing myself or how easily the heart changes.

Now that I realised I was attracted to Mitsuyo Miura and could not help myself, Tadashi Maekawa's letter became a tower of strength to me. Tadashi-san knew about this! He would forgive my fickleness.

Life *was* 'hard and perplexing', just as he had said. But who could really have anticipated that only a year after his death a Christian who looked just like him would appear in my life? Thanks to his great understanding and love for me, revealed in that last letter, I could accept my attraction to Mitsuyo Miura.

By that time Miura-san already knew about Tadashi Maekawa and myself, for the *paulownia* box containing the bone stood by my pillow, wrapped in white, and his photo was beside it. I myself had told Mitsuyo Miura in detail about our friendship. There were no secrets between us. He knew all about Ichiro Nishinaka and my current friends. The only thing he did not know was how I felt about him myself.

But however much Tadashi Maekawa might forgive my fickleness, I was still ill. At long last I was able to get up and look after myself to some extent, but otherwise I lay all day long in the plaster cast and the symptoms of my illness showed little change. Besides, I was now thirty-four, two years older than he was and, needless to say, I was not attractive. I was not fit to love a man or to be loved by him, so how could I disclose my feelings to him?

At that point my family consisted of my two parents and my youngest brother. My father was nearing seventy and frail, and my mother was well into her sixties. My illness had cost them so much money as it was, and just the daily letters I wrote were a financial burden to them. Moreover, if there were many visitors, that also involved the expense of light refreshments, but my mother received them gladly. In spite of the pressure of housework and nursing she would give lunch to those who came near noon and an evening meal to those who came in the evening. And far from grudging me all this she went and visited my sick friends for me. When I tried to thank her she would often say, 'You enjoy having visitors and as long as I'm well enough I don't mind where I go to visit your friends for you.'

She made many close friends among my friends' mothers and those who nursed them. I thought she was exceptional, even though she was my own mother. Tired as she would have been with nursing, she was not one to show it by her expression or words, and my friends said her cheerful, welcoming attitude made it easy for them to visit me. Mitsuyo Miura and his like, especially, said they admired the unfailing welcome of her smile. If my mother, worn out with nursing, had once been ill-humoured, diffident people such as Miura would probably not have continued coming and then my lot would certainly have been very different.

But apart from that, I could not help regretting the financial hardship I was causing my parents, and the way I had to depend on them to do my laundry, however sick I was. Was there no way I could earn some money?

As I thought about it, some wonderful curtains arrived from my sister-in-law. One glance and I decided these had commercial possibilities. I had been lying in bed for so long I knew nothing of the world outside and those appliqué curtains brought in a great wave of fresh air.

When I made enquiries immediately to see if it was

possible to sell them in large quantities, wholesale, they said it was. I promptly discussed the matter with my younger brother. He took an interest at once and undertook to contact the shops on his day off from work.

Hitting on a plan of strategy, we received orders from almost all the well-known Hokkaido department stores. A further request came for typical Hokkaido products. Then I asked one of my regular visitors to sketch out my design. I also devised various new designs and decided to make these myself. But that was all very well, I had no capital and I could not do it all myself, lying down. I needed money and people. Boldly I decided to ask a friend of my younger brother's for 350,000 *yen*[4] as capital, and asked a friend's wife to make the curtains. Fortunately, this lady could do beautiful work. And in addition I got four or five sick friends and housewives to help.

As I lay there I ordered the materials I decided on, one by one from my brother. Then I made a paper pattern and sent it with the material to my friends who made it up. The work progressed better than I had expected and I was able to buy a washing machine and rice cooker for my mother, and every month I was able to give her some money, however little.

And in the midst of it all I was desperately doing my best to try and forget about Mitsuyo Miura.

47

At this point I would like to turn to my diary. Immature as it is, it is an important record for me.

March 2nd: Temperature 37°, night sweat.

I received letters from my eldest sister Setsuko, Miwako-san and Sugawara-san. Wrote to Sugawara-san and Taguchi-san. It's the funeral for Yuri-san's baby. (Yuri is my older sister.) It only lived for fourteen hours.

[4] Then worth £350 or US $875.

A baby born to be buried. By now it is already in the earth. My brother said it was a child to be envied. Yasuhiko-san would certainly have said the same. Those who do not know the joy of living are miserable. One woman who committed suicide asked, 'Will tomorrow be happier than today?', and the question also comes, 'Was yesterday happier than today?'

My own happiness rose to a peak during my five years with Tadashi Maekawa and then crumbled. What am I waiting for now? Nothing but darkness. But as I have given thanks for that time of radiant love I received, so I must rejoice whatever the grief and suffering henceforth.

Now Miura-san's existence is deliverance and light, but not romance. Love! I think that there is nothing but unhappiness for those who wait for that.

My emotional nature is such that I cannot live without a deep, spiritual love. If I have that, I don't need the physical. And moreover, I reject love which is purely physical. Is this because I am still immature? At any rate I'm searching for the deep riches of knowledge, affection and will.

What sort of person am I really? I'm all at sixes and sevens. My thoughts are like elusive dreams. I have nurtured folly and evil and yet I cannot give up my yearning for purity. I'm a romanticist, born in the Taisho era[5], with great faith in mankind. I'm as foul as a woman endlessly floundering in a swamp. It isn't so much a matter of indifference whether I live or die. I feel I would cause less trouble if I were not here. Someone once said of me, 'Wherever you go there's trouble', and I was stupid enough to be proud of it. The truth is, you're not fit to love someone like Miura-san.

'Oh, God, please forgive me for everything. Oh, God, even as I have been filled with your grace today I have been narrow-minded and have not loved others. Please make me loving and kind and generous like my mother.

[5] Emperor Taisho's era: 1913–27.

I commit to you the spirit of that baby who was buried today. Please give me love, real love.'

March 3rd: A cold, temperature 37·2°, sweat.

Letters from Miura, Hirahara and Tanako Saito. So Miura-san has gone on a business trip. There is some emotion in his card. I feel I too am on a journey. My heart goes with him. Is it just the romanticism of travel? It is a long way to Wakkanai. I'm waiting for him to get back safely. I would like to hear his childhood stories from that area.

'Oh, God, today also has been a day when I deserve death. I thank you for all I have sought and received through your grace. It has been a day of coldheartedness, envy and ingratitude. Please have pity on me for Jesus' sake. Emmanuel. Amen.'

March 7th: Letters from Sugawara, Nishimura and Miyakoshi-san. The Hokkaido *Araragi* came. Neither Miura-san nor I have contributed. For some reason I cannot write poetry at present. None of them is any good.

Moreover, I must not associate with Miura-san. I must make myself realise that I cannot make another person happy. That is to say, if I am virtually an invalid, then as an invalid I must renounce all that is in the world. It will still be a long time before I am better. Ayako, you must not forget that you have no right to love anyone. There is nothing about you which another person might love. You must not take advantage of Miura-san's friendship. Miura-san would never do anything under-hand. He is always straightforward — just as he never has a hair out of place and is always correct. He's not the sort of person to give way.

'Oh, God, let me hold your hand and walk step by step with you.'

April 28th: No letters.

I dreamt about Miura-san. He was ill and being carried by some woman. He said he was returning to his home town by train. She was a middle-aged woman with a kindly face. I gazed at her, thinking she must be his mother. The train slowly drew out, and I stood on the platform watching him leave, my heart aching with love.

I wondered whether I would see him today, but I didn't. Tomorrow? But there can be no more love for me. I must not love.

May 1st: A letter from Miyakoshi-san.

Two years have passed since Tadashi-san lost consciousness and died. I've sent his family three packets of rice flour and a letter. In these two years I have never forgotten him for a single day, though I have not been faithful to him alone for those two years. My weak spirit has wavered towards another. But Tadashi-san, I have never forgotten you. In the evening I read his poems.

We loved each other. We went for walks. We went on excursions to the hills. We went to church. We met in coffee shops. We were in the same hospital. We went by train to Sapporo together. We saw films. We worked for the TB Patients' Association. We went to poetry readings. Together we edited poetry. Together we studied. Together we visited sick friends. We were always together and we were brimming over with happiness. I lived for him, he lived for me, and if we could have died together we would have been happy. But never mind. I can still think of no one like you. No one can love me as richly as you did. Thank you, God. Thank you, Tadashi-san.

May 2nd: Temperature 37°, repeated headache and deep sleep all day. The anniversary of Tadashi-san's death. I read his diary.

May 11th: My soul is hungry. It hungers for something intellectual and for deep affection.

I must write some farewell notes. I want to be ready for death. Men wait quietly for death and are not suddenly taken by surprise[6]. I can't do that.

Life is more precious than we think. Have we realised
[6] See note on page 62.

this? I received this life of mine in exchange for Jesus' life. Now I have understood this at last, not just in my head but in my heart. I've grasped the real reason why my life is so precious. Forgive me, Jesus.

My diary reflects my own confused, vacillating heart. In contrast to this, the venture with the curtains found a steadily expanding market, although most of the proceeds were allocated to personal expenses and repaying the loan. However, I did receive some money and felt that even if I were ill for the rest of my life, if I had the will to work, I could at least earn some pocket money. This may have arisen more from my inner sense of desire to remain single for Tadashi Maekawa's sake than from anxiety about the future.

When I lost Tadashi Maekawa, Yasuhiko Mafuji became more concerned for me than previously. He had gone to Hokudai University in Sapporo but sometimes returned to Asahikawa, and then he never failed to come and see me.

One day he suddenly muttered, 'Ayako-san, there's something different about you.'

I was taken by surprise. He knew I was surrounded by many friends, but after Tadashi Maekawa's death he seemed to think he was the closest to me. He had said before, 'If you can just get well enough to care for yourself, I still want to live with you.'

He kept dreaming of how wonderful it would be for a man and a woman to be friends and live together under one roof. But my own heart was vacillating constantly between the dead Tadashi Maekawa and my new friend Mitsuyo Miura.

'You've changed. Something's different.' He looked at me, his attractive eyes searching.

'You've changed too. You've grown up.'

He had finally emerged from being a rather effeminate youth into a mature man. He was twenty-seven.

'Tadashi-san was a good person, wasn't he? He had a much greater zest for living than I have. Somehow I feel death snatched him away in an unnatural manner.'

There was a thin beard on his chin. Suddenly his language
had become adult. But he was as perceptive as ever. He had
sensed immediately that my feelings were no longer devoted
to Tadashi Maekawa. I evaded his question.

'Yasuhiko-san, why do you classify mankind into man
and woman? Can't you consider the theme of mankind as
a whole? Homosexual love is offensive when mankind is
divided into two groups, but instead of rejecting mankind,
isn't it more interesting if we probe deeper into human
nature?'

Yasuhiko Mafuji lit a cigarette and surveyed me in
silence. He seemed to sense that I was running away. I
could not talk to him about Mitsuyo Miura. Perhaps it was
because I felt guilty at loving someone when I was thirty-
four and lying in a plaster cast.

Stretching out his hand to shake mine as he left, he
remarked, 'I'm feeling rather lonely.' As he did so I noticed
a small, narrow scar two centimetres long on the back of his
hand. It must have happened in childhood and it seemed
very strange that I hadn't seen it before.

That night, for some reason, I could not help thinking
frequently about Mitsuyo Miura. And the feeling lingered
that there was no harm in thinking. I was lying in a plaster
cast, I was two years older than he, and I had already loved
someone once before, and now I loved him. What was
wrong with that? After a little while I fell asleep, contented.

48

When God took Tadashi Maekawa away He sent Mitsuyo
Miura to visit me instead, and when Nishimura-sensei was
called to Heaven I was given someone else to lead me in the
faith.

Among the many people with whom I corresponded was
a prisoner who had formerly led a gang in Kanagawa Ken.
He believed in Christ after he was condemned to death for
taking the lives of two men in Atsugi. It is commonly said

that he who is strong to do evil is also strong to do good. This man became a sincere Christian and led many fellow-prisoners to Christ.

One day a letter arrived from him. 'Igarashi-sensei is visiting Hokkaido and plans to go to Sapporo. I have asked him to visit you in Asahikawa. I think he will call at some point.'

I knew nothing about Igarashi-sensei but I guessed he was probably a pastor.

A few days later a letter came from Kenji Igarashi. Using the notepaper and envelope of the Sapporo Grand Hotel, he explained he had flown to Chitose the previous day and asked if he could visit me in Asahikawa. This happened fourteen or fifteen years ago, when hardly anyone used planes.

I was disappointed, because not one of the pastors I knew was rich, and a pastor's work is so poorly rewarded. And yet for all that, this Igarashi-sensei seemed to be wealthy. Nishimura-sensei used to say, 'I can use the money needed for a first-class ticket in better ways, but it isn't a luxury for the sick and the elderly to travel first class.'

I decided that if this pastor could travel as far as Hokkaido then he could not be elderly, and I arrogantly declined his visit.

'I'm not at all well at present and cannot see anyone.'

An answer came by return, 'I won't bother you now, but please take care of yourself.'

After that Kenji Igarashi sent me the Christian magazine *Grace and Truth* every month. For a year I never sent him a word of thanks, so it was not surprising that I was conscience-stricken and finally wrote a postcard to thank him. It was a very simple matter but a letter came by return.

'Thank you so much for reading what I sent you.'

Now he was expressing his thanks to me! It was a very humble letter and I was crestfallen. As I re-read it his character emerged. This was no ordinary person. Ashamed that I had been so conceited, I wrote a second letter and in return he sent me a calendar. It was of various customs around the world and came from the Hakuyosha Cleaning

Company, with the note, 'This is my company's calendar. I hope it will brighten your sick room.'

I'm ashamed to admit it, but I did not know what sort of company the Hakuyosha was. I merely associated dry cleaning with the cleaning shops in Asahikawa. Only later did I discover that this company claimed to be the largest cleaning company in the orient, with shares listed on the stock market. I learned then, for the first time, that he was an old man of eighty and travelled by plane at his own expense. If he were elderly it was acceptable for him to travel by air and stay in a hotel. I had assumed he was a pastor getting help from America, but now I was mollified. Of course I wanted all pastors to have a better status and travel first class by train or plane, but I resented one of them travelling by plane when others were not so fortunate.

At any rate, Kenji Igarashi apparently did not lack money and although I had already realised that he was no ordinary person, child that I was, I wrote to him saying something like this:

'Are you a rich person? I don't find rich people frightening.'

It was a very curious letter. Probably he smiled over it. Gradually he grew fond of me and even said he had acquired a new daughter.

He was a wonderful Christian, in no way inferior to Nishimura-sensei. After working for the Mitsukoshi Company until he was twenty-nine, he had set out to be independent and laid down for himself the following principles:

Not to allow any hindrance to Sunday worship. (His desire to worship at church on Sundays is said to have been his main reason for becoming independent.)

Not to compete in business with Mitsukoshi, who had helped him so much, or to stop giving Mitsukoshi his custom.

Not to utilise a lot of capital.

To dispense with deceit and bargaining.

To benefit people and not harm them.

When Igarashi-san of Hakuyosha read these to me, I

admired them. Mere common sense suggests that it is right to use experience when setting up independently. If you have worked in a drapers you handle such goods; if you have worked in a restaurant you open a restaurant. It stands to reason.

But Igarashi-sensei was different, because he freely gave up ten years' experience and would not choose any work which impinged however slightly on Mitsukoshi's trade. As a result he began this cleaning business.

There is a saying, 'The laundry lives on the dirt of the neighbourhood'. It reveals how much people dislike the idea of a laundry.

Igarashi-san explained, 'Someone like myself with no learning or ability could never draw the crowds in a popular kind of business, so it occurred to me that I should do the work that people disliked, rather than what they liked.'

As he had begun by working in Japan's foremost department store he felt embarrassed at first to be turning to the laundry business. 'But when I remembered how Christ, far from just washing away ordinary dirt, took all the defilement of man's sin upon Himself and bore the disgrace and suffering of the cross, I thought, 'What is so shameful in men like myself washing away other men's dirt? Cleaning is the vocation I have received from God, and I'm going to devote my life to it!'

So he decided, and only a year after starting up he had founded the first dry cleaning business in Japan.

This man came to see me in Asahikawa in June 1957. As I waited I could not but feel that as a result of this meeting I would know what I ought to do about Mitsuyo Miura.

49

It was drizzling with rain when Kenji Igarashi arrived at my home, bringing with him his secretary and the manager of the Sapporo branch of his company, both of them Christians.

Standing beside me as I lay, he gazed at me in sorrow and expressed his heartfelt sympathy. To judge from his alert face no one would have thought he was eighty. I commented that he looked more like sixty. He spread a blanket over me, with a flowery pattern of green and white. It was his visiting gift. Straight away I asked him to pray and sing a hymn. He chose one of my favourites, and with his companions sang out strongly for me,

> Jesus, you love me,
> The waves are surging,
> The wind is howling,
> And I am going to sink:
> Protect me.[7]

Then he opened his Bible and read the story of Jonah from the Old Testament.

Jonah was a prophet. Although he was told by God to go to Nineveh, he escaped on a boat. The boat ran into a great storm with big waves and the other people on the boat decided to draw lots to discover whose sin had brought the storm on them. The lot fell on Jonah. When they heard that Jonah had refused to obey God's command and had run away, they threw him into the sea. But suddenly the sea disappeared, for Jonah had been swallowed by a great fish and was inside it three days and nights until it vomited him on to the land. Jonah then went to Nineveh and prophesied that the wicked city would be destroyed after forty days, with the result that the people of Nineveh feared God and repented. Jonah had prophesied destruction as God commanded, but God forgave Nineveh and saved the city.

Jonah was extremely angry. He was ashamed because it had not happened as he had prophesied. He left the town and made a small hut for himself, and sat waiting to see what would happen to Nineveh. The Lord God expressly *prepared* and raised up a climbing plant to save Jonah from suffering the intense heat. It provided shade over his head.

[7] *Jesus, Lover of my soul* . . .

Jonah was delighted with the plant, but the following evening God *prepared* a worm which made it wither. Soon after
the sun was out, God *prepared* a hot east wind, and when
the sun shone on Jonah's head again he was utterly
exhausted and asked to die. He was angry, but God said 'You
shouldn't be angry. You pity the plant which you didn't
sow or work for, which grew in a night and died in a night.
How much more should I take pity on this city of Nineveh
where there are 120,000 people who don't know left from
right, and their cattle?'

He read to the end and then spoke to me. 'It is something
we can thank God for, isn't it? Our God is a God who
prepares for us. Good things and bad things, He is carefully
preparing them for us. He is *preparing* things which will
ultimately be good even if they appear bad to us. We should
thank him most of all that He is *preparing* everything for us.'

He took a room in Asahikawa and visited Abashiri and
Wakkanai to address meetings, and when he was free he
visited me three times. At last it was time to say goodbye
and as he shook my hand his eyes were moist. Later, when
I had fully recovered, I spoke to him about this time and he
said that he had been thinking, 'poor thing, she only has a
short time left', and his eyes had suddenly filled with tears.

His message about Jonah spoke to me. Everything has
been prepared for us by God. Even this illness was a necessary thing for me, and Miura-san had been prepared for me
too.

God will not give us what we do not need. I trusted God
more deeply and knew that if I simply accepted what He
gave me, all would be well. I had hoped that through meeting Igarashi-sensei I would be shown something definite
about Mitsuyo Miura, and through the story of Jonah I
had found the answer.

However much I loved him, if God had not given him to
me I knew there was no choice. From that time I was able
to believe 'God will certainly give me all I need. If I don't
receive something, it shows that I don't need it'. My earlier
worries disappeared.

50

Although my temperature continued and my tonsils were often swollen, I felt that little by little I was getting stronger.

One fine day at the beginning of July my shoes and clothes were put out to air by the window on the verandah. One of my small nieces exclaimed in astonishment, 'Lying-down-Aunty!' — this is what they always called me — 'These shoes. Whose are they?'

'They're mine.'

'No they're not! You haven't got any feet!'

It was scarcely surprising that she said that. I had been ill from before she was born and she had never seen me standing.

'I have feet too, you know.'

'Really? Then show me; quick, show me!'

'Lift up my quilt and see.'

Half in doubt she turned back the bottom edge of the quilt and cried out in surprise, 'Oh, yes! It's true! You have got feet! Auntie, if you've got feet, why don't you walk?'

'Because I'm ill.'

'Oh!'

As always when she came to my room, she made up stories and sang to me and disappeared again.

I felt so helplessly disabled and crippled, that at this time I was in despair. But there was the comic side too. To talk of an invalid like me loving someone else could only be described as comical. How could I love another person deeply from my heart when I could not even stand properly on my own two feet?

It was not long since I had written down my last wishes, just in case, and put my poems in order. My primary request was that my body should be used for dissection. Sick and useless as I was, I had often heard from Tadashi Maekawa of the shortage of bodies for medical students to dissect, and bodies such as mine, affected by TB in various places, could possibly be valuable for research. At least I could be of some use after I died.

I was never much good at writing poetry. However, being me, I suppose I wanted to leave what I had written to show that I had lived to the best of my ability. Most people want someone to see this aspect of their lives. I was holding the poems in my hand when I suddenly made up my mind to write on the cover, 'When I die, please give these notes to Mitsuyo Miura'.

He was of the same mind as myself and was now a member of the same Araragi Society. He would certainly read my poems and, more than that, he was the one that I now loved best in the world.

At the time it was definitely my intention that he should see them after my death, so I don't know why I handed the notes to him one day. He raised his eyebrows slightly as he looked at the cover and, taking a knife, neatly removed the phrase 'when I die'.

'You're going to get better!' His voice was stern, but then he smiled gently.

He took them home and read them immediately, and was deeply moved by my poems of grief for Tadashi Maekawa. He even said that the most beautiful love poem among them was,

> You held me in your arms as if I were your wife.
> Oh, come back, come back from Heaven.

He also said that until he read it he thought all women were fickle, but these lines had changed his views.

I was candidly revealed in those poems. Many of them were about the love between Tadashi Maekawa and myself. Mitsuyo Miura was touched, and because of my faithful love for Tadashi-san his own feelings toward me deepened.

Another day dawned beautiful and clear, like the day when we had first met. I was sitting up in bed gazing out of the open window and as the large roses started to open I had a feeling that something good was going to happen. I shall never forget that 19th day of July. A bulky envelope was delivered from Mitsuyo Miura.

'I dreamed that you had died and I prayed to God with tears for over an hour. My eyes were still swollen when I went to work.' And the word 'dearest' was written over my name.

I re-read the letter. What I was waiting for had come at last. I left my hand over the word 'dearest' and tried to quieten my trembling heart, I was so happy. It was an indescribable happiness, but at the same time the thought came, 'Is this all right?' Firstly I was ill and had no idea when I would get better. What sort of happiness would he get from loving me? He was already past thirty. How many years might he have to wait for me? Gradually my rejoicing changed to a feeling of heaviness. Even if I got better, would I be able to bear him children? I recalled his poem:

> I want to remain single all my life,
> But the desire to be a father creeps back.

For a long time he had intended to remain single, not only because he had had one kidney removed. He may also have wanted to devote himself heart and soul to his faith. And maybe he did not want to involve himself too deeply in a world full of evil. Then there was his distrust of women. Yet at the bottom of his heart the desire to become a father remained. When I considered all this, I had to exclude myself, in my present state. What was love all about really? I picked up a pen and wrote a letter.

'Miura-san, your letter was so totally unexpected that I don't know how to answer it. When I read the word "dearest" I had no simple feeling of joy or unworthiness. I felt faint and I could not have stood up if I had tried.

'I did not want you to love me as a woman, because that would mean unhappiness for you. Miura-san, I'm ill. I haven't a single way to make you happy. I hope you will fall in love with a healthy young woman and marry her. Miura-san, I was happy when I could just love you in my heart. I was glad you were alive.

'I read your letter in tears and wept as I prayed. If God lets me love He will heal me, but as I am now I cannot hope to return to even half a normal life. Miura-san, because I truly love you I cannot bring myself to encourage you to marry a sick woman. Ill as I am, I don't know how much of a burden I might be to you.

'Maybe you have never yet met anyone you could love, because your heart was closed to all women, but now you feel like this, try making friends with girls at church or at work. I'm sure you will find a healthy, attractive, good-natured girl worthy of your love.

'O God, please help us both to be strong in the Lord and to love You. If it is Your will, please give us a pure love in the Lord and fellowship together all our lives. Please show us clearly, Lord, the path we should follow, and please forgive me for my confusion. I believe the way you have prepared for us is the highest and the best, in Jesus' Name, Amen.'

I want to share with you I John, chapter 4, verse 12, 'No man has ever seen God: if we love one another God abides in us and His love is perfected in us'.

Ayako

To Mitsuyo Miura.

It was a letter of eleven pages.

But nonetheless I was weak. I could not follow my reason and reject his love completely, and before I knew what was happening I could no longer hand him over to anyone else.

51

One day one of my pupils who worked in the same Forestry office as Mitsuyo Miura came to see me. She was looking through my photo album when she suddenly stared and exclaimed,

'Sensei, do you know Miura-san?'

'Yes, because we're both Christians.'

I asked her what Miura-san was like at work.

'He's a very quiet person. He spends his lunch hours by himself reading books. There is something unusual about him. One of my friends has lost her heart to him and says she would like to marry him.'

She was apparently ignorant of our relationship. It certainly never entered her head that the man that her girl friend was pining for might be attached to her former teacher. With the words, 'Everybody has lost their hearts to him,' she left.

As I thought over what she had said I was reminded again that someone of my pupil's age would be far more suitable for him. It was unfortunate that he should love someone two years older than he was and sick into the bargain. So when he came to see me later I said, 'Miura-san, could you have fallen in love with me out of sympathy or a feeling of gallantry?'

He shook his head emphatically and said quietly, 'There is no hint of mere chivalry or pity in my feeling for you. There are plenty of attractive girls in the office, at church and at home. But I love you instead for the beauty that has come to you through your suffering.'

'But when I am ill like this you can't marry me even if you love me.'

He replied immediately, 'We'll get married when you are better. If you don't get better I shall remain single.'

How wonderful it was to hear that! I was utterly overwhelmed with gratitude. But there was one more thing I had to speak frankly about.

'Miura-san, I shall never forget Tadashi-san.'

As usual I had the *paulownia* box containing Tadashi Maekawa's bone by my pillow and his photo beside it. I could not forget him. He had not turned his back on me and gone away. He had stood on the deck of the ship of death watching and waving to me as he gradually departed, and I had stood on the quay waving until I could see him no longer. However much I waved he would never come back now and, though I knew that, I could not stop waving. As I stood there I had suddenly been joined by Mitsuyo Miura. He resembled Tadashi Maekawa so closely in his face, his faith and his thoughts that the resemblance had made me hesitate again. Couldn't I go on loving Tadashi Maekawa through Mitsuyo Miura? I knew it was out of the question, and yet the thought would not go away. Mitsuyo Miura spoke.

'It is important that you don't forget Tadashi-san. You mustn't forget him. You became a Christian through him. We've been brought together through him. Ayako-san, our life must be such as would make him happy.' His eyes glistened with tears.

I stretched out my hand and clasping it firmly he prayed, 'O God, please let Your will be done. Please purify and lift up our love.'

52

From that time Mitsuyo Miura only came to see me on Saturdays, so his visits were not particularly frequent. He usually stayed about an hour and never a long time. It was not unusual for some of my friends to go on chatting for three or even four hours, so sometimes I would complain, 'Miura-san, you go home sooner than anyone else.'

But he refused to be moved by pity and would answer, 'I don't want to be a nuisance when you're ill'.

When he came, he would enquire how I was, read the Bible, sing a hymn and discuss something with me for a while, such as our faith or poetry. And when the time was up we would pray together and he always went home apparently unconcerned.

Maybe it was because he had been ill a long time himself that he was so constantly concerned about the fatigue caused me by visitors. Even when we shook hands he was afraid I would exert too much strength. He constantly seemed to be urging me to devote all my physical strength to fighting the disease.

One day he brought me this verse, written on a card:

To have faith is to be sure of the things we hope for,
to be certain of the things we cannot see[8].

He put it in a frame himself to encourage me, and when we met he would cheer me up with the words, 'You're definitely getting better.'

Was that why I gradually grew stronger, although I had not been outside for a long, long time? I recovered enough to see him off at the front door, and naturally by this stage I could do much more for myself. How can I describe my delight when I first went to the bathroom alone? Even when I was able to walk a little I could not bend at all, probably because of the long time I had spent in the plaster cast. Dizzily I practised, repeatedly, until my joints loosened up, and I was overjoyed. I went almost tearfully, wondering how many years it was since I had opened the door, and rejoiced that I would never again need anyone to nurse me.

I often reflected on how much I had taken for granted before, when I was well. No longer did I treat everything as a matter of course. Walking and standing were no longer everyday things. How many handicapped people there must be throughout the country! Bed-ridden people who lie there day after day, longing only to be able to stand on their own two feet and go where they will.

Little by little I reached the point where I could sit up for meals. Until then a tray of food had been placed on my chest as I lay prostrate and I had to eat by seeing the food reflected in my mirror. It was so wonderful to be able to look directly at the dish before my eyes. I almost trembled for joy. Sometimes even now I suddenly think, 'I can look at my food with my own eyes as I eat!'

It is fearful to grow over-familiar with things and I am afraid lest I inadvertently forget those vivid initial impressions.

[8] Hebrews 11: 1 (TEV).

I remember a friend coming to see me when I was prostrate and saying, 'The moon is beautiful tonight. Shall I show you?'

Taking two mirrors she tried to help me, but we could not catch it in my hand mirror. She did all she could, until suddenly despair swept over me and I said, 'Never mind, thank you.'

But when I was able to leave the plaster cast and stand and gaze at the moon and stars from the verandah I wanted to cry out,

'What beautiful things there are in the world!'

I could not bear the thought that anyone failed to notice the beauty of the night sky, when so many people throughout the world are forced to spend their lives in bed.

53

In this way my friendship with Mitsuyo Miura continued undisturbed, until one day, when the snow was beginning to fall, he had to go to another area on business for ten days.

When he returned he brought me gifts of a bookmarker and fruit, and at the same time drew a letter from his pocket. I took it without thinking and was startled to find it written in a beautiful feminine hand.

He explained, 'I brought it because I don't think we should hide anything from each other, however small.'

At his urging I started reading. For a long time she had admired him, and the beauty and reality of her affection was revealed in skilful sentences. I was thrown into confusion. This healthy young woman would surely be a suitable companion for him. A mere glance at the contents of the letter amply revealed her femininity and intelligence. Moreover, she had accurately assessed Mitsuyo Miura's character and respected him.

I asked bleakly, 'Have you answered it?'

'No, because it was waiting for me when I got home last night.'

She must have been waiting over a week to hear from him, wanting an answer whichever way it was. Mitsuyo Miura spoke again.

'I always believe in the principle of closing the door before the wind blows. I hadn't mentioned you to her.'

He left saying he would tell her about me. I wondered whether he would really be able to. Be it man or woman, it is a wonderful thing to be loved by someone else, and whichever way I looked at it I could not help feeling that she had so many advantages over me. This alone made me fear for his reaction. And then I hated myself for giving it even half a thought. Miura was not a fickle person. I should know that better than anyone. I was ashamed of having doubted him even a little.

A few days later he brought a second letter from her. It was genuine and sincere.

I understand you are waiting for someone who is ill. Please excuse me for my rudeness. I'm earnestly praying that she will recover as quickly as possible, so that you can both be happy.

I was touched, in fact deeply moved by Mitsuyo Miura's attitude when he informed her about me, without hiding anything, and by hers in being able to write such a letter to him. At the same time I felt that I owed her an apology. I could not help wondering how often one unwittingly wounded others and made them suffer. If I had not existed I would not be pushing this girl aside, and Miura[9] might then have married her. What a humbling thought, that inescapably we influence the lives of others by our very existence. Nevertheless, Miura was a very eligible bachelor and received many proposals. Even when a senior colleague at his office to whom he was indebted suggested someone to him, he firmly declined, saying, 'The matter has already been settled'.

---

[9] The honorific suffix *san* is dropped as she is now referring to her fiancé.

Whenever I think of him answering so positively and with such dignity, although he had no idea when I would recover, I still recall that deep feeling of gratitude and happiness, that came over me.

54

My room was as crowded as ever with friends, men and women. Usually we talked about the Bible and sometimes we sang and prayed together. I see in my mind's eyes one medical student, who had only been a Christian for two months, sitting Bible in hand. He is still an earnest believer today. Whether it was my response to Mitsuyo Miura's love and encouragement or to the friendship of so many, I gradually became stronger until it was possible for me to go out.

But for some reason or other, in the autumn of 1958 I began to have hallucinations. When I woke up and my eyes were open I could see red and green objects like Chinese ornaments in the air. One time there was a cow's face, another time a Buddhist altar. It did not last long, but it was unpleasant.

A doctor I knew strongly urged me to go to the psychiatric department of Hokudai University Hospital, but I hesitated. It would be the eighth time I had gone into hospital and I had caused my family enough trouble. Yet I wanted to go, for although I was better my temperature still did not return to normal. If I were going to marry Miura I would need a detailed investigation of this at least. As it was unpleasant in hospital during the cold winter, I decided to wait until it became warmer the following year. In the meantime I thought I could save up a little money by making curtains. Both Miura and the doctor said they would pay my medical expenses, but I wanted to avoid troubling them as much as I could.

In July 1959 I was admitted to Hokudai University Hospital in Sapporo again. As I had been bed-ridden for so long, I should by rights have been very pale, but all the time my face had kept a light tan. To my friends it was remarkable, considering I had not been out in the sun for years. Some of the hospital doctors rather foolishly suggested that I had not been in bed at all. But my own doctor wondered if there were some adrenal disorder, so I decided to have that investigated too.

Of my eight times in hospital this was the happiest. Instead of complete rest I could walk up to two hundred yards, and did not need to ask the nurse for anything. So I was really happy. But I found one thing strange, when I went to the bathroom each morning. No one chatted with anyone from a different room. In fact no one even said 'Good morning'. They gloomily brushed their teeth and washed their faces. It seemed so miserable to begin the day like this when they were able to look after themselves. So I took to greeting them in a loud voice with 'Good morning!'

Not a single person greeted me back. The next day I said it again, and again nothing happened. Undaunted, I greeted them each morning and at long last, a week later, one person returned my greeting. 'Thank goodness,' I thought, and seizing the opportunity I asked, 'How are you?'

From that day on you could sense the complete change in the atmosphere. Soon the first class patients were mixing with those from the wards, and after the evening meal those who were well enough visited each other's rooms. There were all kinds of sick people there, but none had been ill as long as I had. I think the longest was six years and that was only half of my twelve. Simply because I had been ill so long, I think, people gradually began to feel their own illness was not so bad after all. And I was glad that my own experience could become a source of encouragement to others.

Daily I racked my brains for something, anything to make the others cheerful. If they could forget that they were sick, then just for a little while they were not patients. In the evenings some of them would come asking for 'a talk about God' and while I spoke quite a number always gathered round my bed, listening attentively. My heart ached to see those earnest faces, and I came to realise that everyone, no matter who, was seeking for something.

Happily there was nothing abnormal in my encephalogram, my temperature went down and the colour of my face became normal. Through all this period Miura never stopped sending me encouraging letters and part of my hospital expenses. Thanks to him I was able to stay in hospital longer than I had expected and get well again.

When I had been there previously I had not known a single person. Now over a hundred people were coming to see me. They were almost all companions in the faith which I had found when I had been in hospital before. Of course, at the bottom of my heart there was still a touch of loneliness, as was only to be expected at the university hospital where Tadashi Maekawa had studied, the hospital we had attended together as patients. Nishimura-sensei, who had visited me more frequently than anyone, was no longer among my many friends. I could only pray that I might comfort other sick people as Sensei had done, and love them as Tadashi Maekawa had done.

After some two months in hospital I went home and my parents and Mitsuyo Miura were waiting for me.

55

Back in Asahikawa I told my family and Mitsuyo Miura the results of the detailed investigation. It was a miracle that the cavity, with the haemorrhages which had made me fear death so often, had now completely healed — and my spine too, thanks to seven years' lying patiently in a plaster cast. But as the tuberculosis had also given me some gynaecological problems, I continued receiving heat treatment at the Asahikawa hospital and the daily visits gradually restored my strength. I had been under six stone, and before I knew it I was over eight stone.

The New Year of 1960 came. Miura was the first to call, so together we read the Bible, sang hymns and prayed. Then

I said, 'You must pay me a New Year visit like this next year too.'

He stopped in the middle of eating Abekawa rice cakes, his chopsticks poised, and silently shook his head. I gazed at him, astonished. 'Why not?'

Smiling gently he answered, 'Next year, let's pay our New Year visit here together.'[10]

'What? Together?' I caught my breath. No words could describe the joy that filled me.

When he had gone I told my mother what he had said. At the evening meal she spoke to my father.

'Father, we'll have to buy a chest of drawers this year.[11]

'A chest of drawers? Why?'

'Well, it's Aya-chan. She says she's getting married!'

'Aya-chan getting married? Who on earth is the fellow?'

My father never made jokes. His daughter had been bed-ridden for many years and even now spent the greater part of each day in bed. And she was thirty-seven. Even my own father could not imagine that anyone would want to marry a person like me. It was inconceivable. No wonder I'm still overwhelmed by the depth of Miura's love.

'Miura-san has said he wants to marry Ayako!'

My father looked blank and said, 'But look here, surely Miura-san is married already.'

Many men, married and single, had been coming to see me, and Mitsuyo Miura was thirty-six that year. From his age and mature manner he probably looked happily married. When he knew it was real my father had to blink away the tears. The three of us sat lost in our own thoughts, our chopsticks lying there forgotten.

On January 9th, Miura's older brother arrived to discuss the matter formally. It was no small thing for him to accept me as his brother's bride. If my younger brother had waited

---

[10] The more cultured the Japanese are, the more indirect their language becomes. This is a reference to the formal New Year calls paid to one's parents after marriage.

[11] Traditionally the bride provides linen and a chest of drawers for her new home.

to see whether someone older than himself would get better or not I would almost certainly have said, 'Your dream may never come true. Why don't you marry someone else before you get too old?'

Actually, my doctor opposed our marriage. He was afraid I could not stand up to it physically. Then a certain pastor said, 'Now look, marriage is real. It's no good dreaming about it.' Even perfect strangers warned us, in view of my condition and out of concern for Miura. It certainly caused quite a stir. But apparently his older brother said, 'If you marry the person you love, you will both have achieved your desire even if one of you dies three days later.'

Having lost his father in childhood Miura looked on his older brother as a parent, and his generous words of advice were a great encouragement to us both.

The engagement ceremony was fixed for January 25th, a Sunday. At that time engagement ceremonies were held in our church with all the members present. We took our vows before God and the pastor prayed for us. Then, instead of engagement rings we exchanged Bibles to indicate that we would be guided by God's Word all our lives. When the ceremony was over we paid a formal visit to the house of our 'go-between', my own pastor and his wife from Nijo church, to tell them what had happened.[12]

> The falling snow changed to hail and rain as we
>   walked through the town.
> From today you are my fiancé.

The weather that day was quite extraordinary. The snow was driven sideways by wind unusually strong for Asahikawa and, as we watched, it turned to rain and then to hail. Somehow the bad weather suggested many hardships ahead of us. Then I glanced up at the sky and was taken by surprise. In spite of the wind, snow, rain and hail around us, the sun

[12] Even when marriages are not the result of formal introductions, friends are asked to undertake the position of 'go-between' in all the arrangements.

was shining brightly through the clouds. I recalled Nishimura-sensei's words, 'The sun is always shining above the clouds', and I knew it was true. We could not tell how much bad weather lay ahead, but however bad it was, above the dark clouds the sun would always be shining. The snow would go, but the sun never would. Our God was our Sun and I firmly resolved never to lose sight of Him, for I felt that He would lead us both through the clouds, and I was happy.

56

The wedding was arranged for Sunday, May 24th, but two weeks beforehand my temperature suddenly rose to 39°C. Miura had said repeatedly, 'You don't need to worry about anything. We can use the mattresses we've slept on up till now',[13] but even so I had done my best to get everything prepared. The doctor gave me injections, but without effect. When three days passed and then four I became uneasy. There were only ten days now until the wedding. What if my temperature stayed up?

Day after day wedding presents and mementoes were delivered from my sick friends all over the country, with whom I had corresponded. Relatives sent me a triple mirror and a chest of drawers. As I lay surrounded by these things I was all the more worried. We had already sent out the wedding invitations and the preparations had all been completed, but this unaccountable fever remained. My father and mother were anxious.

Looking at the chest and the triple mirror I recalled what I had read in the Bible, 'You will be given all that you need.' If God had not approved of my marriage to Miura surely I would not have been given these things. But although I believed this, after ten days my confidence evaporated. Even

[13] Traditionally the bride and her family provide new mattresses made at home with cotton wadding.

if I returned to normal in the remaining four days, I would never have the strength to go through with the ceremony. Maybe this marriage was not God's will after all. I began to get discouraged.

In the midst of all this, Miura was the only one who remained calm.

'We're definitely going to have the wedding as planned. God brought us together. Let's trust Him.' His words were full of confidence.

When he called in to see me on his way home from the office each day he never once appeared worried.

There were two days left. At last my father suggested sending a cable to distant relatives, postponing the ceremony. I had caused my parents trouble right to the end! I agreed with his suggestion, but Miura assured us that everything was all right. Even so, I was still uneasy. What would happen about the wedding if I could not get up on the day? What would people do, especially those who had made long journeys? The more I thought about it the more worried I became.

In the event, Miura's confidence was justified. The day before the ceremony my temperature disappeared without trace. It was nothing but a miracle. And although I had had that fever for ten days it was as if my physical strength had suddenly been released and the weariness disappeared completely. My parents were overjoyed and I was all the more ashamed of my lack of faith. I had forgotten the sentence in the Bible, 'Therefore do not throw away your confidence which has a great reward.' Maybe God knew that complete trust in Him was the thing that I would need most in marriage. I had forgotten this and spent the days rushing around, absorbed with material things so that He had to send this fever to teach me a lesson. I had been facing the wedding relying on Miura's faith, and I could only feel ashamed.

57

The morning of May 25th dawned at last. An unusually
strong wind had been blowing for days and the Asahikawa
wind in May is cold. A wedding dress would be very chilly
in such weather and I was concerned, but from early morning it was fine and warm with no trace of wind. Sick as I had
been so recently, the beautiful day seemed almost to
envelop me with its warmth.

As the church echoed to the wedding march we quietly
entered together and moved up to the front. Then the hymn
which we had chosen was sung by the whole congregation.

> We know not how or what our path will be.
> The Lord will work His will in us.

The bridegroom was thirty-five, the bride thirty-seven.
For that reason alone it was different from most weddings,
but everyone knew of my long sickness. Apart from our
families many of my friends were there. Rië who had once
attempted suicide, the doctor who had opposed our marriage, the pupil who had sent money to me anonymously
when I was sick, the friends who had visited me so often, the
people who had helped me make the curtains and the mother
of the dead Tadashi Maekawa who had brought me to
Christ. How varied their thoughts! What memories they
must have had as they gave us their blessing!

Sometimes a bright light dazzled us. To celebrate my
release from so long an illness, Tsutomu Kuroe, the former
patient, now a fellow Christian, was filming the ceremony.

'Will you love your wife, will you love your husband, in
sickness and in health?'

As we eagerly gave our assent, I thought, 'Isn't that a
vow for healthy people?'

Mitsuyo Miura had never once seen me healthy. He had
loved me as I lay prostrate and helpless in a plaster cast day

after day, with a bed pan nearby. He had loved me deeply when I was ill and had been waiting for me five long years. Deep gratitude made me humble. I sincerely wanted to be a good wife to him and made my vows before God with the earnestness of a child.

The reception was in the hall below the church, a simple affair of cake and tea. The hundred and twenty or so guests completely filled the place and surrounded us with affection.

My pastor was the first to greet us. He said he wanted the reception to end as soon as possible, as neither of us was strong. After that came speeches, and before long Tadashi Maekawa's mother stood up.

'Ayako-san, we congratulate you. We never dreamed the day would come when you would be well like this. I don't know what to say. It's nothing but a miracle . . .'

Her voice trembled and broke. I looked up startled. Her eyes had filled with tears and she bit her lip, overcome with emotion. Softly I buried my head in my bouquet and, as so often before, could see the figure of Tadashi Maekawa bowing over and over again as he went away. Those who knew of my friendship with him certainly understood his mother's tears.

Deep in my heart I whispered, 'Thank you, Tadashi-san. I have married Miura-san.'

I remembered Rië's words, 'Aya-san! Tadashi-san may be the one who rejoices most at your wedding.'

Then I thought of the wedding gift from Ichiro Nishinaka which my mother had handed me the previous night. How wonderfully faithful my friends all were — and Mitsuyo Miura more than any of them. In spite of my unworthiness, God had given me such love and guidance through so many people.

That night, a small buffet dinner was provided for the family. It was after eight o'clock when Miura's elder brother and brother-in-law escorted us to our new home, a reconstructed storehouse with only one room of nine *tatami* mats and a kitchen four mats in size. As Miura later wrote,

When I stretched out my hand I could touch the
  ceiling,
There was only one room, in our first home.

The other end of the roof is the neighbour's
  storehouse;
There is the clatter of wooden shoes . . .

The neighbour's outhouse is beyond our wall.
Late at night there is the sound of falling wood.

But it did not matter to us.

When the two men had gone home, I knelt in front of
Miura, my two hands on the *tatami,* bowing low in formal
greeting.

'I'm not much good at anything. Please be patient with
me.'

Miura formally returned the greeting and then together
we offered a prayer of thanks to God from the bottom of
our hearts.

As we had sung in the hymn that day, we could not
fathom anything about our future, but we prayed that
whatever happened, we would both stand firm in our faith
and live sincerely.

It was a warm spring evening without a breath of wind.